THE

PRINCIPAL'S

HANDBOOK

ON THE SCHOOL LIBRARY MEDIA CENTER

BY

BETTY MARTIN

AND

BEN CARSON

with a foreword by Dr. Gordon Cawelti

Gaylord Professional Publications
Syracuse, New York
1978

© Betty Martin and Ben Carson 1978
First published in 1978 by
Gaylord Professional Publications
Syracuse, New York 13221

Library of Congress Cataloging in Publication Data

Martin, Betty, 1910-
The principal's handbook on the school library media
center.

Bibliography: p.
Includes index.
1. Instructional materials centers.
2. School libraries. I. Carson, Ben, 1932-
joint author. II. Title.
Z675.S3M735   021'.24   78-1957
ISBN 0-915794-22-5

CONTENTS

4

FOREWORD

Someone once defined the great teacher as the person who is able both to help organize knowledge for the student and to interest the student in the teacher's subject. Many teachers fall short of meeting this kind of definition because they have failed to recognize the impact of the "visual literacy" phenomenon. Almost from the start of the formalized study of the educative process, philosophers, researchers, instructional theorists and indeed Marshall McLuhan himself have advanced that it is crucial that visual depictions accompany the abstractness of print material when maximum impact is to be made in teaching important concepts in all subject fields.

This book makes an important contribution to those who would attempt to seriously deal with the visual literacy phenomenon by providing practical advice to instructional and administrative personnel who are responsible for the curriculum in a school. As the book points out, many schools have transformed their library to what is termed a "media center" but in fact it remains essentially a place for the storage and retrieval of predominantly print material. It is fundamental to the change process that one realizes that any substantive change in the parts of the system changes everyone's role and the promulgation of a media center is no exception to this observation.

I feel quite strongly that instructional leaders need to work much more seriously at introducing "power" into the educative process. It does little good here in the last quarter of the twentieth century to lament the addictive character of television and its subsequent impact on the learning habits of young people. This electronic invention has already induced in most youngsters what one might call a requirement for a visual stimulation before true learning occurs. Thus, it seems to me that we need to capitalize on this and turn the use of visuals to better instruction in the school subjects.

I don't believe that the development of a media program means in any way an abandonment of reliance upon print material. This book in no way implies that and clearly we will need to continue to need the efficiency of printed material as a primary learning device. The important contribution that this book makes is to develop a more comprehensive approach that assures broad utilization of all materials in the center by providing a better understanding of role implications for principals, teachers, superintendents and the media specialists. If understanding and commitment are deficient among any one of these persons, the media program will fall short of its potential impact on the instructional program.

The authors' many years of experience as an administrator and media specialist comes through as they argue quite persuasively for early and continuous participation on the part of the media specialist in curriculum planning. This problem continues to plague media specialists who are brought in after the fact and thus are unable to provide assistance in curriculum development activities. Again, unless the incumbents in all four roles outlined clearly understand this, it is extremely difficult to have a strong and pervasive media program.

I strongly believe that any principal or superintendent who is seriously interested in extending the utilization of a media center, or is interested in simply getting a media program underway would do well to use this book as a starting point for developing a plan of inservice education to clarify the role problems which are most often the chief deterrent to affective media programs. Quite clearly this would be of invaluable assistance as a starting point in attempting to provide that "power" so badly needed to compel the attention of the young learner in today's schools.

Dr. Gordon Cawelti
Executive Director

Association for Supervision
and Curriculum Development

PREFACE

This joint effort in authorship by a media services consultant and a school administrator has been made to acquaint principals with the concept of a library media center and their role in the establishment and optimum functioning of such a resource.

This book is designed to be used as a reference tool which principals may consult to find the specific information needed or to answer one or more of the questions which serve as chapter headings. These are questions which have been asked most often by the principals during the combined fifty-one years of public school experience of the writers. Interrelationships between questions necessitate some repetition of facts.

Principals are the key persons in the development of exemplary school library media programs. Because they are responsible for their school building programs, and because a fully functioning library media center is a vital ingredient of a superior school program, it is essential that principals be knowledgeable about all facets of the media center and their broad implications. Without the principal's support and leadership the strong media specialist falters and the weak one is lost. In both situations the school program and the children for whom it was designed, suffer. School principals who both understand the philosophy and support the implementation are needed to develop school media programs which are a basic driving force for excellence.

The attention of readers is called to the fact that hereafter the shorter term "media center" will be used instead of the more descriptive "library media center." Numbers within parentheses refer to bibliography entries.

The writers greatly appreciate the many helpful comments and suggestions offered by the following during the preparation of the manuscript of this book:

Dr. Mary Edna Anders, Head, Basic Data Branch, Industrial Development Division, Engineering Experiment Station, Georgia Institute of Technology.

Mrs. Mary Frances K. Johnson, Professor of Library Science, University of North Carolina at Greensboro.

Mrs. Margaret W. Ehrhardt, Library Consultant, South Carolina State Department of Education.

Miss Mae Graham, retired, formerly Assistant Director, Division of Library Extension, Maryland State Department of Education.

PART I

THE MEDIA PROGRAM AS A COMPONENT OF THE SCHOOL PROGRAM

1

WHAT ARE THE GOALS AND OBJECTIVES OF THE MEDIA PROGRAM?

Before assuming a commitment to a media program so vigorous that it vitalizes the total school program the principal wants to know the goals and objectives of the media program. These goals and objectives are a reflection of the educational philosophy of the school district and the purposes and intent of the superintendent, the principal, the school staff, the students, and the parents. A knowledgeable visitor to a school can quite accurately estimate the principal's educational goals by observing the library media program. Prostano and Prostano quote Emory's contention that "school libraries, developed for the educational program of the school, tell more about a superintendent's philosophy than any other department or area of the school."([32]) The same observation applies to the principal, and his/her philosophy.

Some educators are confused about the distinctions between philosophy, goals, and objectives. In 1907, the California Governor's Task Force on goals and objectives for public education set the following definitions which are quoted by Stoops, Rafferty, and Johnson:

"Philosophy means a composite statement of relationships between the individual and society based upon the beliefs, concepts, and attitudes from which the goals and objectives of the school district are derived. 'Goal' means a statement of broad direction or interest which is general and timeless and is not concerned with a particular achievement within a specified time period. 'Objective' means a devised accomplishment which can be verified within a given time and under specified conditions which, if attained, advances the school system toward a corresponding goal."(39)

As an example of the relationship between the goals and objectives of the media program and those of the school district consider the following:

SCHOOL DISTRICT	MEDIA PROGRAM
Philosophy	*Philosophy*
The belief that those in a school community should work as a team in promoting educational progress.	Same
Need	*Need*
The need for staff, students, and members of the school community to participate in curriculum making.	Same
Goal	*Goal*
The principal will set up groups composed of teachers, parents, and students to work on curriculum revision and to develop special projects.	A continuous program of teacher-media specialist-student-parents planning to revise the media skills instruction.
Objective	*Objective*
By the end of the school year the group working on the social studies curriculum will have developed individualized materials.	By the end of the school year 50% of the media skills instructional materials will be individualized by teacher-media specialist-student-parents planning.
(Additional objectives will be needed to implement the goal.)	(Additional objectives will be needed to implement the goal.)

The educators in some schools prefer not to state all objectives in behavioral terms. Some objectives in the affective area are

14

difficult to state in that way and precise assessment is hard to achieve. In whatever way objectives are stated the fact remains that it is important for them to *be* stated. The media staff needs to know where they are going and how, and what progress they have made.

The media program goals stated below are based on the educational philosophy that:

Education should be learner centered.

Students learn at various rates and have different learning styles.

Each student should be given opportunities to develop to his or her potential intellectually, culturally, socially, and personally.

Each student should acquire the skills, attitudes, and concepts to enable him or her to function adequately in society.

Student self-direction in learning should be fostered.

The goals of the media program shaped by this philosophy are:

Adherence to a continuous process of setting up and revising objectives and evaluating progress.

Development of user-centered media services.

Close cooperative planning between media specialist and other members of the school staff.

Fostering the flexible use of the media center and easy access to a wide variety of media and services.

Promotion of skills of locating, selecting, and using media effectively.

Guidance to students to become increasingly self-directed and independent in learning.

Promotion of student competencies in communication skills.

Fostering of aesthetic appreciation and pleasure in reading, viewing, and listening.

Administering of the media program in such a way that optimum implementation of the school program is achieved.

Other media program goals which are in the affective area are:

— Development of student decision-making skill.

— Fostering of the perception that failure in an endeavor stimulates the exploration of other alternatives for learning.

— Promotion of a positive self-image.
— Development of joy in reading, looking, and listening.
— Promotion of ability to value different kinds of competencies in others.

After media program goals are established, objectives are developed to implement each goal. A number of such objectives are required for each goal. The following is one goal with a partial list of objectives.

Goal:

Consultation of media staff with teachers and students to promote skills in locating and selecting media and in using these materials effectively for their purposes.

Objectives:

By the keeping of accurate records it will be ascertained at the end of a six weeks period that the media specialist consulted with each teacher once every two weeks on the teaching of a media skill.

After each student has completed the use of an individualized learning package on the skill of using encyclopedias 70% of the students will be able to locate a specified piece of information correctly in two different sets of encyclopedias.

After a class, in small groups, has been instructed in the skill of notetaking 60% of the students will be able to take accurate notes on a textbook selection.

There are a wide variety of other objectives which would be needed to implement this goal, e.g., objectives related to media center orientation and organization, media skills, utilization, and production. Examples of the goals of the media program and related behavioral objectives are contained in publications issued by the Santa Barbara High School District and the Oakland Public Schools.

It can hardly be overemphasized that it is unrealistic to expect the media program to support and to strengthen a school program and to contribute to the fulfillment of the individual student's potential if these programs are addressed to implementation of divergent goals and objectives. As societal needs change and educational emphases shift to meet these changes, new school organizational patterns and instructional methods are developed.

Sometimes there is a lag in corresponding alteration and modification in the goals, objectives, and programs of the media center. This results in ineffective and unproductive use of media resources and affects the quality of learning. Administrators should monitor carefully the media program in their schools to be sure that it has kept pace with the current instructional goals and practices. It is stated in *Media Programs: District and School*, "The media program exists to support and further the purposes formulated by the school or district of which it is an integral part, and its quality is judged by its effectiveness in achieving program purposes."(25)

BASIC RESPONSIBILITIES OF PRINCIPALS IN THIS AREA:

TO ENSURE THE FORMULATION OF GOALS AND OBJECTIVES FOR THE MEDIA PROGRAM WITHIN THE CONTEXT OF THE SCHOOL GOALS.

TO INCLUDE THE MEDIA PROGRAM GOALS IN SCHOOL PROGRAM DEVELOPMENT.

TO ASSUME LEADERSHIP IN FOSTERING THE PARTICIPATION OF STAFF MEMBERS IN IMPLEMENTING THESE GOALS AND OBJECTIVES.

SCENARIO

West Elementary School opened in 1977; yet, it would be difficult to prove that it was not just a well maintained facility that opened in the early 1960's. With the national current stress on individualized instruction, flexibility and involvement in education, the instructional program at West is textbook oriented in a rigidly disciplined environment. All the students use the same material and they are expected to learn in the same way and at the same rate. Innovations, often referred to as frills, are frowned upon. Parent suggestions, along with those of students, are disregarded.

The media specialist at West hears a different drummer! It is the desire of this professional to plan with teachers, to provide services for students according to their needs and to have a flexible media program. At the beginning of the year in order to accomplish these goals, he developed objectives to bring about the desired changes. Very little progress was made and this lack of progress was reflected in the yearly report.

Questions:
1. At West Elementary, things might have gone differently if . . . Discuss the variables; list them. Then decide on plans to bring about needed changes.
2. Could the traditional library be altered to fit the existing school program and yet have elements of flexibility and innovativeness?
3. Might the media specialist have done anything to improve the situation—the school program as well as the media program?

2

WHAT IS THE DIFFERENCE BETWEEN A TRADITIONAL SCHOOL LIBRARY AND A MEDIA CENTER?

After a principal understands and accepts the goals and objectives of the media program the question arises, "How shall we bring about the change from traditional library to media center? What is the difference?"

These are questions which have been on the minds of many administrators, expressed by some and unexpressed by others. Though it is difficult to generalize, the term "traditional library" refers to many school libraries in the pre-1969 era, and to many today which are still functioning as they did.

A program to move libraries toward ideal media centers was described in the American Association of School Librarians' 1960 publication, *Standards for School Library Programs.*(3) Though implementation of this program was slow at first, it later was accelerated by rapid changes in education and technology and by federal funds provided for increased materials and facilities.

The new terminology for libraries and expanded services was first sanctioned by the American Association of School Librarians and the Department of Audio-Visual Instruction of the NEA in the 1969 publication, *Standards for School Media Programs.* The term "Media" was defined as "all forms and channels of communication."(2) Note well that *books* and other printed materials are included. The media center was described as a learning center

19

which stocked all types of media and provided access to media and services for members of the school community. A media specialist was defined as a person who has been prepared professionally to administer these media, and to plan and deliver services as an integral part of the instructional program.

At first, administrators had two misconceptions concerning the new terms. Some thought that they were just new names for the old library and the "old" librarian. Others thought that, if they added some filmstrips, disc recordings, and a few pieces of equipment to the library collection, they would then have a media center.

The 1975 publication issued by the American Association of School Librarians, ALA, and the Association for Educational Communications and Technology, *Media Programs: District and School* delineates guidelines for media programs and resources essential for quality education.(27)

It must be pointed out that in some schools the libraries have been upgraded to include most or all of the media center features hereafter mentioned but the principals and school staffs have elected not to use the new terminology. This is evident in some of the quotations used in this handbook. The writers believe that the substantive quality of the media program, not the terminology, will determine the impact upon the school program. It is this essence of a revitalized learning center which will be explored here. The use of the terms "library" and "media center" facilitates communication when describing changes which have taken place.

The concept of a true media center differs from that of a traditional library in six dimensions: program, personnel, facilities, collections, administration and financial support. Superintendents, principals, teachers, students, and parents need to realize the potential of this new concept of their schools' centralized resources for learning. This is particularly essential for administrators. Ward and Bacon believe that "the administrator is the electric link between effectiveness or failure of the instructional media program."(42) Principals, in particular, need to understand that, to transform the traditional library into the vital resource it should be, changes should be made in the areas mentioned above. These changes will be described briefly in the following pages and contrasted with the program and procedures of the traditional library. Later chapters will include a more detailed analysis of these six dimensions of the media center.

It must be emphasized that *program* is the most crucial of these areas. It is after all the product of the interaction of all the other ingredients. It is possible that the changes hereafter described could be made in all other aspects—personnel, facilities, collections and the rest—but if the program remains limited and deficient then the goal of a top-notch media center will still not have been achieved.

In looking first at program, it is noteworthy that from the meager and restricted traditional library services experienced in many schools, the media program has expanded into every facet of the school program. The media specialist has become a valued partner with the teacher in curriculum development. The media program includes:

Setting objectives and evaluating the media program.
Meeting individual needs and working with small groups.
Continuing cooperative planning with other staff members, individually or in small groups.
Increasing the use of non-print materials.
Assisting teachers and students in the production of materials.
Assisting teachers and students in designing learning packages and developing learning centers.
Teaching curriculum related media skills.
Providing services tailored to the needs of atypical students, e.g. the gifted, the underachievers, the handicapped, the culturally different, and the "non-media-users".
Efficiently organizing and circulating media in many different formats—throughout the school building and into the students' homes.
Maintaining a receptive attitude toward new media and innovative teaching techniques.
Directing and coordinating the contributions of volunteers.
Being actively involved in all aspects of the school program.
Implementing cooperative activities with community agencies, i.e., public library, Red Cross, pollution control agency, institutions of higher education, etc.

In addition to the expanded services listed above, increased emphasis in the media center is placed on staff development and inservice education activities. Because the utilization of a good media program and improved learning opportunities depends

21

upon receptive, cooperative, knowledgable teachers and other staff members, they are given help in understanding the range of media services, in upgrading their media skills, and in enhancing their professional competencies.

Library services in the tradtional library were often limited in several respects. Except where there was a particularly energetic, knowledgable librarian, service was given only to those teachers who visited the library and/or requested services. Seldom was there an active sustained stimulation of those less inclined to library usage. Usually the librarian was not included in the curriculum-making process, did not plan regularly with all teachers, and was not involved in curricular activities. Skills were taught, but too often they were unrelated to curriculum or student needs. Elementary library services were trapped within a rigid schedule for each class and this dictated the program. Also, services did not include circulation of non-print materials to students for home use. In the traditional libraries many librarians struggled valiantly to give good service even though their libraries were understaffed, understocked, and undervalued.

The areas of personnel, facilities, and equipment will be discussed in detail later and are mentioned only briefly here.

In the area of personnel, the difference between the library and the media center is obvious. To carry on the range of services described above, the staff of the media center must be larger and more specialized than that of the library. The publication *Media Programs: District and School* recommends one fulltime media specialist for 250 students. "A ratio of two fulltime support staff members for every 250 students (or major fraction therefore) is recommended to fully implement a well-developed media program, . . . based on analysis of the tasks to be prepared and the time required to perform them."(27) Support staff members are defined as media aides and media technicians. In this publication recommendations are also made for schools with larger enrollments.

To some administrators the number of media staff members recommended seems beyond all reason, but the need for such a staff is understood by those who have observed or experienced the extent and diversity of the media program and have seen its impact on the total school program. However, numbers of staff alone do not guarantee a good media program. The competencies of the staff are an important consideration when deciding the number needed.

It "makes a believer" out of a principal to see media personnel working with other staff members frequently, to find the media center usually filled to capacity with students purposefully using media of all types, to observe much work of the media personnel with students on a one-to-one or small group basis, to note a high circulation count of all media, to enjoy the sound slide or other productions of students and to observe the contributions of media personnel in instructional design, curriculum planning sessions, and in inservice education activities.

Number, however, is only one aspect of the media staff when compared with the library staff. Expanded services require media personnel that are fully qualified educationally for the work they do and with personal characteristics that include being out-going, innovative, flexible, armed with inter-personal communication skills, and knowledgable about curriculum processes and newer media.

In the traditional libraries, except for large high schools, the program limped along with one professional librarian. Some conscientious librarians devoted excessively long hours after school and on weekends in order to accomplish necessary tasks. Others limited services to teachers and students in order to take care of administrative duties during the school day. The librarian could hardly play a significant role in the learning process.

The change from a library to a media center also involves changes in facilities and equipment. Space allocations must be larger and more diversified to provide for the wider variety of activities. Use by individual students and especially by small groups, increases when stimulated by a fully-functioning media program. A sizeable amount of audio-visual equipment requires space and a larger production area is needed with the addition of production to media services. The well developed media center program will probably require different kinds of furniture too. More individual study carrels should be provided and more spaces for small group activities.

As to collections, it has already been pointed out that the media center is the focal point for the acquisition, organization, and circulation of all manner of non-print materials in addition to the basic library collections of materials in print format. Though traditional libraries often had (at least in recent years, with the advent of Federal funds,) a respectable collection of books, periodicals, newspapers, and pamphlet materials, the media center stocks an even wider variety and also large collections of equipment, filmstrips, audio-tape and disc recordings, slides, transparencies, video tapes, study prints, posters, maps and globes, 8mm films silent and sound, models, games, toys, and in some cases 16mm films. The efficient media specialist organizes all of the media so that they can be easily accessible to teachers and students.

Differences are also found between the administration of the media center and the old style library. The media center features a warm, welcoming climate; it is run *for,* not *in spite of,* the students. Excessive and restrictive rules governing its use have been eliminated and this is conducive to an enjoyable informality. Rather than prescribed "one-at-a-time" whole class visitations there is encouragement for many small group or individual student activities according to instructional needs. Innovative ways to use media are welcomed. Non-print materials are considered equally with printed media as a selection is made to meet instructional objectives. Teachers and students understand circulation procedures are not meant to be a barrier to the use of media to achieve their purposes. Students as well as teachers are allowed access to files to select the media they need. The media specialist promotes the wide circulation of both print and non-print materials. While excessive noise is not condoned, students feel free to move around and discuss their work with others as they use various media. Teachers and students feel that this is *their* media center. They assist in the selection of new media, make suggestions to solve problems, or serve on the media committee, and students serve as assistants. Students know that the members of the media staff are concerned about their progress and they regard the media center as a comfortable, satisfying place to visit to find new, exciting and highly individual ways of learning.

The administration and media staff are alert and receptive to the potential of new media in varied formats. They investigate or instigate contractual arrangements with computer networks.

They promote district or regional centralized cataloging facilities and collections of costly materials. They keep informed about any new administrative practices which may promote a more vigorous media center.

The sixth area of differences between the traditional library and the media center focuses on financial support. It is obvious from the differences in other areas noted above that the funds allocated for a media center need to be substantially greater. For two many years the traditional libraries existed anaemicly on a starvation diet. As long ago as 1948 Walraven and Hallguest advocated practices which are considered desirable in a modern media program. (41) However, during the following years many of these suggestions were not implemented and this was often due to limited funding. Even today state and regional standards for allocations for school media prorams are unrealisticly low. The supplementary funds of the first federal programs provided the transfusions which revived libraries. Principals in their planning for excellent media programs should set as a goal the recommendation cited in *Media Programs: District and School* which is 10% of the current National Per Pupil Operating Cost. (27)

If the administrator understands and becomes enthusiastic about the ways in which the media center differs from the traditional library in the six areas of program, personnel, facilities, collections, administration and financial support, he can successfully provide the "spark" and the guidance to facilitate implementation of the changed concept among teachers, students, and parents. Rowell emphasized this: "It is his (the superintendent's) interpretation of the program to himself, his staff, his board, and his community that will both initially and ultimately light up the land—or blow the fuse."(35) The principal shares this responsibility. It is a wise administrator who monitors and guides the development of the media program so that the total school program will reflect and respond to new power.

BASIC RESPONSIBILITIES OF PRINCIPALS IN THIS AREA:

TO BECOME AWARE OF THE SUBSTANTIVE DIFFERENCES BE-
TWEEN THE TRADITIONAL LIBRARY AND THE MEDIA CEN-
TER.

TO BE INFORMED ABOUT THE CHARACTERISTICS OF AN EX-
CELLENT MEDIA CENTER.

TO BECOME KNOWLEDGABLE ABOUT STRATEGIES FOR MOVING
FROM A TRADITIONAL LIBRARY TO A MEDIA CENTER.

FIGURE 1

SUMMARY

Traditional Libraries

Program:
Schedule classes rigidly
Assist students with reference work
Teach library skill sets to given whole classes on a routine basis whether they relate to other learning or not.
Have story hours for whole classes
Help individuals find a "good book" to read
Promote little use of non-print materials
Provide materials to teachers as requested
Allow media to be thought of as "enrichment" of learning rather than basic to it.

Personnel:
Usually limited to one professional or one professional and one media aide.
Schools with enrollment of 1,000 or more add another professional.
Note: Though limited, an exceptionally competent staff often develops a good media program.

Facilities:
Elementary schools usually have space large enough to seat one class plus 10 or 15 students.
Few if any spaces suitable for individual or small group activities.
High schools—space to seat 10%-15% of students, 1-2 conference rooms, a few carrels.
Small storage and work spaces.

Collections:
The bulk of the collection is printed materials.
Usually, collections of filmstrips and disc recordings are available in small quantity.
Acquisition of media is limited to cer-

Media Centers

Program:
Formulate objectives within context of objectives of school program
Hold conferences with teachers and other school personnel on a continuous basis to design learning activities
Work usually with individual students and small groups rather than with whole classes
Promote extensive use of non-print materials
Promote freedom of access to media center and flexibility of use
Teach media skills as need is indicated
Engage in total involvement in the instructional program
Have "story hours" structured to needs of small groups
Participate in implementation of new instructional techniques
Identify non-users and plan activites to meet their needs
Promote wide use of community resources
Evaluate media program on basis of objectives
Select the materials— print and non-print— which best meets user needs

Personnel:
Progress toward goal of 1 media specialist, 1 media aide, and 1 media technician for every 250 students as services expand.
Note: The quality of the staff is as important as the quantity. Numbers alone do not assure a good program.

Facilities:
Provision for individual and small group activities.
In both elementary and high schools space to seat 30%-40% of enrollment.
Three or more conference rooms, listening rooms, dark room, etc.
30% space used for carrels.
Ample work and storage spaces.

Collections:
Extensive collections of all types of media are available for circulation to teachers and students.
A flexible policy is maintained toward adding new media as they are issued, and needed.

FIGURE 1 (cont.)

SUMMARY

Traditional Libraries (cont.)	*Media Centers (cont.)*
Collections (cont.)	*Collections (cont.):*

Traditional Libraries (cont.)

Collections (cont.)
tain times—perhaps once or twice—during the school year.
The professional tried to do everything—including all acquisition and processing tasks.

Administration:
Austere, formal atmosphere
Many rules and regulations to govern use
Emphasis on quietness
One whole-class acitivity at a time
No circulation of non-print materials to students for home use
Non-print materials and equipment often not easily accessible
Little input by teachers and students in selection of new media or administration

Financial Support:
Minimal

Media Centers (cont.)

Collections (cont.):
Tasks are assigned to support staff, and much material is centrally or pre-processed.

Administration:
A warm, friendly, informal atmosphere
As few regulations as possible
Flexible and innovative use encouraged
A variety of activities carried on simultaneously
Circulation of all media to students for home use.
All materials and equipment organized for easy accessibility
New media selected by media specialist, school, staff, and students
Affiliation with a computer network
Suggestions on administration from teachers and students encouraged

Financial Support:
Adequate support and recognition of need to increase allocations as program expands.

SCENARIO

A principal decides he is going to develop a media center in his school. He has visted and observed media centers in other schools of a comparable size to his, approximately 2,500 students.

He remodels the traditional library space to increase the size, to provide spaces for different size groups, and to provide an adequate workroom, office, and storage spaces.

He purchases additional audio-visual equipment and appropriate furniture.

He employs additional professional and support personnel and increases the library budget.

He then waits for the metamorphosis from library to media center to occur. He's disappointed when not much happens.

Questions:
1. What cardinal principle of change did he overlook?
2. To which other areas should he have directed his leadership?
3. When he realizes his mistakes, what steps should he take?

3

What Is the Relationship of the Media Program to the School Program?

Principals are aware that the media program is a component of the total school program and that in working to develop the media program they are engaged in implementing overarching instructional goals.

Particular features of the relationship may be illustrated by comparing the school program to a plant and the media program to the soil in which the plant grows. The nutrients in a rich soil are assimilated into every stem and leaf of the plant, make it strong and flourishing, and become part of the plant. In much the same way, an excellent media program extends into every department of the school, strengthens each teacher's instruction, and becomes part of the total school program. Without fertile soil the plant is undernourished and stunted. Without a stimulating, extensive media program, the school program is inadequate and sterile. Because a properly functioning media program blends into the overall school program, a more precise term for this relationship is "interrelationship." This interrelationship might be characterized in terms of three adjectives: *close, continuous, cooperative.*

Media services are closely interwoven with every facet of instruction. One example of this is seen as the instructional program or components of the program are planned or revised. Figure 2 provides a schematic presentation of the process; its first

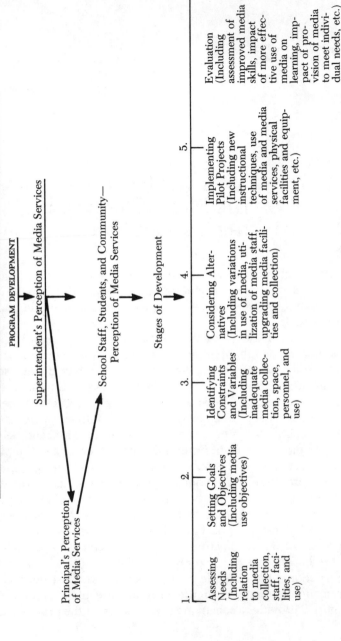

FIGURE 2

INTERRELATIONSHIP BETWEEN MEDIA SERVICES AND THE INSTRUCTIONAL PROGRAM

30

FIGURE 3

THE INSTRUCTIONAL PROGRAM

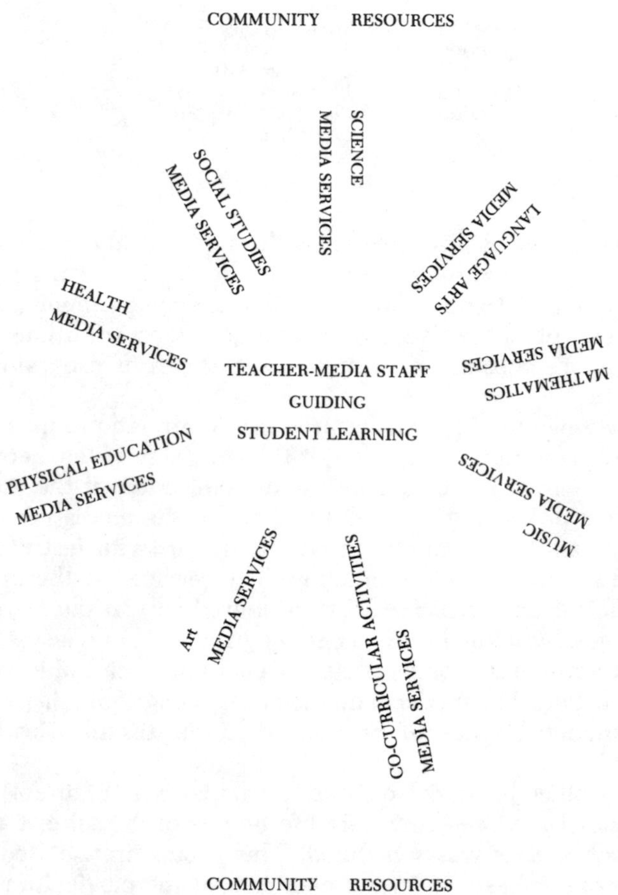

COMMUNITY   RESOURCES

SCIENCE
MEDIA SERVICES

SOCIAL STUDIES
MEDIA SERVICES

LANGUAGE ARTS
MEDIA SERVICES

HEALTH
MEDIA SERVICES

TEACHER-MEDIA STAFF
GUIDING
STUDENT LEARNING

MATHEMATICS
MEDIA SERVICES

PHYSICAL EDUCATION
MEDIA SERVICES

MUSIC
MEDIA SERVICES

Art
MEDIA SERVICES

CO-CURRICULAR ACTIVITIES
MEDIA SERVICES

COMMUNITY   RESOURCES

items need some explanation. Basic to any integration of the media program and instruction is the perception of the administration and school staff that the role of the media program is fundamental to effective learning.

FIGURE 4

TRADITIONAL PATTERN
THE INSTRUCTIONAL PROGRAM

Period I	Social Studies
Period II	Mathematics
Period III	Language Arts
Period IV	Library Acitivities
Period V	Physical Education
Period VI	Music/Art
Period VII	Science/Health

Understanding of this role comes through verbal communications and actions that spell commitment flowing from superintendent to principals to school staffs, students, and community. As a result, media objectives, strengths, weaknesses, contributions, and evaluation are considered during all the stages of program development.

Instructional program-media program interrelationship is also observed in the implementation of the program. If teachers are making extensive use of a good media collection, if the media specialist is promoting services fully, and if the media center is freely accessible, the media program merges with instruction. Figure 3 illustrates such interaction. The services of the media program in each curricular area are ingredients in the learning experiences. Individual students, small groups, whole classes, and teachers consider the media program a necessary part of learning and instruction. The media center space is thought of as a part of the instructional space to be utilized in the teaching-learning process.

On the other hand, in the traditional pattern (Figure 4) the library may have been considered to be one of the subject areas into which a class was scheduled. This procedure isolated the library experiences from other elements of the curriculum and limited the impact upon the students' learning. This practice is still seen in some elementary schools.

Besides having a "close" quality, the interrelationship also has a *continuous* one. Media services do not function as a "sometime thing" in instruction. The use of the media center by teachers and students is not peripheral in instruction. Some teachers have been known to make use of the media center only occasionally as a diversion while "real" instruction was centered in the textbook or special classroom materials. Some media specialists, on the other hand, have been known to plan the program of the media center independently of other instruction. The media program which is operating correctly has an every day, all day role in the life of the school. The media professionals, fully conversant with all curricular areas, teaching styles, students and learning abilities are the common resource for everyone in their building. The principal builds and promotes this ongoing resource by referring to it in meetings and in conversation with individual teachers, students and parents and by using it himself!

The media services - instructional program interrelationship is also a *cooperative* one. Cooperation characterizes any joint operation or team effort. In some schools only the media specialist is working hard to encourage teachers to join in activites designed to ensure the more effective use of media. Cooperation makes the successful program "go". In a truly cooperative interrelationship both parties join in a shared effort to work together for a productive learning environment.

Swarthout calls attention to the fact that "cooperative planning sessions must be involved wth the real matters of curriculum and the problems of student learning."(40) This means that teachers and media specialists must study, originate, and plan together. Sometimes this planning is an indepth development of a learning unit at the beginning of a study topic; sometimes this is a less inclusive conference during the study. They pool thoughts, plans, and competencies as they consider the following areas:

Goals and objectives of proposed study
Topics, concepts, skills to be introduced
Special student interests, needs, and learning levels
Available relevant materials
Effective ways to use these materials according to study content and student needs
Identification of media skills deficiencies and planned instruction

Planning of learning sequences, design of learning packages and learning activity centers

Evaluation procedures and the design of evaluation instruments

As plans are implemented the teacher and media specialist continue their cooperative activities. The teacher interprets to students the most productive use of media, and works with students and the media specialist in the media center as well as in the class area. The media specialist, equally at home either in the classroom or media center, introduces students to resources for information retrieval, works with the teachers to teach and re-teach skills as needed, sharpens awareness of the values of reading habits and the continuing use and evaluation of media, and guides students in the evaluation, organization, and critical analysis of the information they have gathered.

The services of the media specialist go far beyond the academic aspects of the program such as English, Mathematics, Science and Social Studies. Other instructional areas - music, art, physical education, health and the like—benefit greatly from media program support and collaboration. It is also essential and a natural outcome of a fully realized media program that the media specialist provide services to those involved in such activities as inter-scholastic athletics, school newspaper and annual, student government, special projects, community-school affairs (i.e., citizens advisory councils, parent-teacher associations), the guidance program (i.e., student-teacher advisory system, career planning, counseling), and the range of clubs and varied activities which function as a part of school life.

Examples of the functioning of the program in areas other than the instructional program might include the following:

— The media staff works with the faculty sponsors and students on various club programs
— The media technician and a group of students make a sound-slide program on school activities for a P.T.A. meeting
— The media specialist and technician arrange a bulletin board display on the work of the student council
— The media staff meets with the counselors to evaluate the behavior and work habits of several students

34

— The media staff helps a steering committee of students plan a school election, make posters, write speeches, design a bulletin board display, make a video-tape
— The media staff helps the yearbook committee find background material on space flight which has been selected as the theme for the year
— The media staff assists several school departments as they participate in a community fair; such contacts are a form of public relations which help shape attitudes about public education.

The principal should assess the quality of the media program as it is operating in all areas and provide guidance in helping it broaden and deepen its effectiveness. The attitude that the media center is an extension of every other learning space station and situation, and that the media specialist is a partner in all the efforts of the staff is projected by the principal. Such a concept is reinforced and nurtured by the principal. Whether or not the media center, its program and the media specialist's services are fully utilized and completely productive, depends in large part on the principal.

In assessing the media programs in their schools, principals should place high value on a close, continuous, cooperative interrelationship between media services and the school program. To expedite this they provide the facilitating climate, flexible school organization and administration, continuing staff development, time for joint planning, and of course the media resources which are essential. They also give to teachers and the media staff the guidance and the counsel which provide inspiration, motivation and problem-solving assistance. The media specialist must provide services to numerous groups - professional, student and citizen. The informed leadership of the principal is imperative!

BASIC RESPONSIBILITIES OF PRINCIPALS IN THIS AREA:

TO UNDERSTAND THE INTERRELATIONSHIP OF THE MEDIA PROGRAM AND THE SCHOOL PROGRAM.

TO BE AWARE OF HOW THE MEDIA PROGRAM AND THE TOTAL SCHOOL PROGRAM CAN BE UNIFIED.

TO ASSUME A LEADERSHIP ROLE IN THE IMPLEMENTATION OF AN INTERRELATED PROGRAM.

A principal assumes a position in an elementary school of 450 students. She finds that the curriculum and teaching methods are traditional, the achievement levels are low, and there is no provision for individual differences. Some of the teachers discourage innovations. The discipline is unusually strict. There is a large group in the community interested in improving the school.

The principal finds that the librarian has set up a rigid schedule for use of the library - one hour per week per class. Except for a few students who come to the library before and after school, students always come to the library with a class group. At their assigned time the teacher *sends* the class for the activity which the librarian has planned for them. Other than class instruction the librarian spends most of her time cataloging materials, circulating books and shelving books. There are only a few recordings and filmstrips which are used only by the teachers. The librarian doesn't utilize student assistants because she says they make too many mistakes and things must be kept in order.

Questions:
1. Is this library program suitable for the school program?
2. Where should the principal begin in response to community pressure for improvement? Who should be involved?
3. How should objectives for the library be formulated?
4. How should the principal function as a change agent?
5. Should an effort be made to implement a full program of media services?

PART II
DEFINITION OF ROLES

4

What Is the Role of the Principal?

Since the effective media program is so truly a part of the overall school program, the principal, other members of the administration, and the teachers have important roles to play in it as well as do members of the media staff.

There are three major conditions that apply to these roles. The first of these is that they are interrelated and function in unison. A person in one of these roles does not operate unilaterally. The second requirement for the most productive fulfillment of these roles is that there should be a common commitment to the goals of the media program, a perception of how it is operated, and how much it can contribute to an exemplary school program. The third general condition for successful performance in these roles is continuing easy communication. It is difficult not to discuss the roles of principal, teachers, and media specialist all at the same time since they are so closely affiliated; however, for the purpose of clarity they are considered separately here.

Since the principal is the key person in providing a framework and a climate for implementing the media program, this role will be explored first. Because the media program permeates the whole school program, in no other area is a facilitating climate more essential. It is the principal who must create this climate. He or she does this by providing encouragement and stimulation of wide use of media, support for diverse and innovative ways of using media, and the comfortable knowledge that failure will be accepted as part of growth, part of the process of improving practices. A good group spirit promotes cooperative assessment of progress and the planning of alternatives to achieve goals. A prerequisite to the establishment of this type of climate is a perception among staff members that the principal has a genuine interest in and appreciation of the media program's vital contribution to the learning process. Ward and Bacon quote an interview with the principal of an outstanding elementary school, "I view my learning center as the focal point of the school and plan my classroom observations, consultation with teachers and analysis of the needs of children with this in mind."(42) If the staff is fully aware of this attitude on the part of the principal its members will be receptive to cooperative efforts to use media services effectively.

Cooperation is impossible without good, open communication. The principal sets the stage for the productive relationships by indicating ways, times and places in which the teacher and media specialist can make personal contact. An example is set for others if the principal plans a personal schedule which permits time for teachers, media specialists, or students to seek guidance, support, or counsel.

In addition to establishing a favorable climate and communication channels and processes, the principal has other responsibilities in shaping a dynamic, viable media program. High priority should be given to fostering the integration of the media program with classroom teaching and learning and other activities in school and community. The principal must see to it that the media specialist is involved with the staff in planning, in continuing staff development and in evaluation. The principal provides time for continuing periodic teacher-media specialist planning, with individual teachers as well as with small groups, such as high school departments, elementary grade-level groups, or groups working on special projects. The principal who routinely assigns students to the media center so that their teachers can plan together (but without the media specialist) is either ignorant of how much the media specialist can contribute to an instructional planning session or chooses to ignore this added benefit. This practice can help defeat the concept of the media center as a learning center which supports instructional objectives.

Swarthout points out that "to implement both instructional capabilities of the school library and the instructional role of the school librarian, school staffs should plan cooperatively."(40) She also warns that "no in-depth planning occurs at after school or lunch hour staff meetings." Scheduled conference times within school day hours will require some changes in teaching schedules, and teacher assignments, but principals who have made the effort to provide such conference time have been amply rewarded by increasingly wide use of all types of media and more creative learning experiences. When teachers and media staff plan together they can help clarify each other's goals, share competencies, cooperatively design individual and/or group learning activities, and provide an integrated approach to learning opportunities and problems. For example, when the media specialist and teacher work together on a unit on rocks, the teacher receives information concerning needed media skills instruction for groups in her class. The media specialist knowing the teacher's plans for the proposed unit of work can indicate how the media skills may be taught as they are needed. The media specialist makes suggestions for the unit context and assists the teacher in developing a learning activity package for a particular group. Together they plan some challenging activities for other groups. The media specialist offers to assist in the evaluation by observing student media skills and work habits. During the discussion, the media specialist alerts the teachers to books, magazine articles, filmstrips, a forthcoming educational television program, 8mm loop films, and pamphlets on the subject. An offer may be made to secure an exhibit on rocks and a speaker on the unit.

Another way in which the principal can foster a fusing of the media program with the school program is by constantly interpreting, suggesting and illustrating interrelationships to teachers, students, parents and in some instances to those media specialists who have not kept informed about changing educational practices. Rowell believes that "negative or indifferent teacher attitude is due to a lack of understanding of what the media program is, what it can do to support the instructional program, how its resources can be directed to student use, and what those services and resources are."(35)

Inservice education or staff development activities planned by teachers and media specialists can benefit both. Teachers become informed about media services and materials and the media skills which their students should acquire. Media specialists become more knowledgeable about teachers' instructional goals, methods, and needs. Care should be taken to plan inservice education activities carefully. The following guidelines were developed by the Instructional Media Committee of the American Association of School Librarians:

GUIDELINES FOR INSERVICE EDUCATION

Any good inservice education program for the school staff, supervisors, or administrators has certain definite characteristics.

Whatever is planned or whatever is done, an inservice program on the use of media must be considered in terms of its impact on and worth to the instructional program existing in and projected for the school system.

Important principles of operation and organization are:

The program must grow out of problems that are significant to teachers, media staff, supervisors, and principals.

The concerned persons must be involved in planning the inservice activities.

Clear and specific goals such as the following selected potential ones must be set up and kept in focus.

Those participating in the inservice program will acquire information about:

—The roles of media specialists, teachers, and administrators in an excellent program of media services.

—The whole range of media and the operation of equipment.

—The value of planning continuously with media specialists.

—The integrated use of print and non-print media.

—The cooperative teaching of research skills.

—The provision of many opportunities for students to learn to become self-directive in using the media center.

—The planning of ways to encourage students to develop a habit of reading.

—The promotion of student skills of viewing, listening and media production.

—The evaluation of the usefulness of various media to achieve specific instructional purposes.

There must be opportunities for all concerned to share effective techniques that are learned and materials that are located.

Necessary resources, materials, and consultants must be made available. Any program must start where the group is and go as far as possible. Each person must have a vital part in making the program successful. There must be evaluation of progress and re-examination of needs at regular intervals.

After the objectives of inservice education have been developed and the areas for focus have been identified the principal and Inservice Education Committee need to select the group activities to implement objectives. Some activities are more productive than others for particular objectives. Figure 5 lists a variety of activities and specifies those suitable for certain purposes. A selection from this list while planning may prove more desirable than a trial and error method.

FIGURE 5

INSERVICE ACTIVITIES TO IMPLEMENT	PURPOSES OF INSERVICE EDUCATION CURRICULUM
Seminars Large group presentations Lectures Use of resource person Educational telephone network Television series	Understanding of role of the school in society
Seminars Large group presentations Lectures Use of resource person Educational telephone network Television series	Knowledge of curriculum
Seminars Large group presentations Television series Workshops Buzz sessions Brain storming Experiments Use of resource person Reality simulation Models Educational telephone network	Understanding of human growth and learning
Role playing Workshops Reality simulation models Small study groups Seminars	Self-acceptance and acceptance of others

43

FIGURE 5 (cont.)

INSERVICE ACTIVITIES TO IMPLEMENT	PURPOSES OF INSERVICE EDUCATION CURRICULUM
Seminars Experiments Demonstrations Television series Workshops Field trip Video-tape recordings Buzz sessions Brain storming Use of resource person Reality simulation models Educational telephone network	Understanding teaching methods and techniques
Seminars Experiments Small study group Brain storming Buzz sessions Role playing Use of resource person Reality simulation models	Skill in problem solving techniques
Seminars Small study group Workshops Video tape recordings Role playing Experiments Use of resource person Reality simulation models	Skill in group processes
News letter Small study group Workshops Videotape recordings Buzz sessions Brain storming Role playing Reality simulation models	Communication skills
Small study group Workshops Buzz sessions Brain storming Role playing	Skill in problem identification
Demonstrations Television series Small study group Educational telephone network Workshops Field trips Video tape recordings Media Consultants	Knowledge of instructional materials and their use

In addition to cooperative planning and inservice education activities, there are other ways in which the fusing of the media program with the total school program may be promoted. The principal, as a result of observations in classrooms, should point out to teachers during conferences the many opportunities available for using relevant media services providing examples from his classroom observations. Also, during staff meeetings the media specialist should be given frequent opportunities to publicize various features of the media program. Another procedure which fosters media-overall program integration is the appointment of a media services committee composed of teachers, students and parents who meet with the media specialist periodically to plan the program, set goals and priorities, evaluate and consider problems. It is a good practice to appoint a teacher as chairperson of this committee.

Another responsibility of the principal is to give parents and other members of the community a better understanding of the media program. For this purpose the principal should utilize conferences, parent visits to the school, PTA programs and the local radio and television facilities. Sound-slide or sound filmstrip programs can give a vivid picture of the many ways that media services are used in the school.

The principal should expect and let it be known that he expects the media specialist to find ways in which to publicize the media program to students, teachers, and parents. Bulletin board displays and exhibits, assembly programs, the school paper and local press are only a few. Multi-media presentations are very effective for assembly programs.

Another facet of the principal's role in the media program concerns relationship with the media staff. This will be discussed fully in a later chapter. At this point only a few general observations: that the principal should know the number of staff members that are required to maintain a quality media program; that he should recognize that some duties require media aides or technicians while other services require professional personnel; and that he should *never* expect those in either category to perform the duties of the other lest he threaten the proper functioning of the media program.

Additional responsibilities of the principal which are also discussed in other chapters concern adminsitration of the media center, and facilities.

What are the media specialist's perceptions of the role of the principal? The media specialist needs the strong support of the principal in carrying out the media program. In addition, the principal's guidance and counsel and visible support stimulate confidence and provide direction.

THE MEDIA SPECIALIST EXPECTS THE PRINCIPAL TO:

ACCEPT THE CONCEPT OF THE CENTRALIZATION OF ALL INSTRUCTIONAL MATERIALS. The media specialist is able to promote extensive use of all available materials when they are on the media center inventory and in the circulation records. Centralized circulation decreases the need for duplication of materials and assures maximum use, but this does *not* mean that materials cannot be available in classrooms and at other stations throughout the school building.

DEMONSTRATE AN UNDERSTANDING OF A GOOD MEDIA PROGRAM. As the media specialist plans activities with the teachers, the principal's support and help in implementing these arise from a sound grasp of the role of excellent media services in a school program.

PROVIDE LEADERSHIP IN PROMOTING WIDE IMPLEMENTATION OF THE MEDIA PROGRAM TO IMPLEMENT OBJECTIVES OF THE SCHOOL PROGRAM. Teachers will use the media center to good advantage when the principal as well as the media specialist suggest instructional practices which involve media center use.

PROVIDE TIME FOR TEACHER-MEDIA SPECIALIST PLANNING. Often teachers and media specialists say they cannot find time to meet together. They need guidance from the principal and help in arranging suitable times. Some principals schedule periodic planning times.

SECURE FINANCIAL SUPPORT TO DEVELOP AN EXCELLENT COLLECTION OF MATERIALS AND EQUIPMENT, IMPROVED FACILITIES, AND ADEQUATE PERSONNEL. The principal should serve as an advocate in confering with the superintendent, stating the needs and justifications. The superintendent might advise involving the parents in an effort to gain their support for increasing budgeted allocations.

PROVIDE A SCHOOL ORGANIZATION WHICH ALLOWS FREQUENT ACCESS TO THE MEDIA CENTER. This means flexibility in use of the media center, access to the media center for specific purposes during class times, and ease of access before and after school.

RECOGNIZE THE COMPETENCY OF MEDIA SPECIALIST AND TEACHERS TO SELECT NEW MATERIALS. It is a wise principal who relies upon the advice of the media specialist and teachers when considering the purchase of additions to the media collection. Though a principal may have liked certain books as a child they may not be the best purchases today. A teacher's past experience in using non-print materials often proves valuable when selections are made. The principal should beware of succumbing to the lure of the new beautiful expensive set of reference books without consulting the media specialist.

APPOINT A FACULTY-STUDENT ADVISORY COMMITTEE TO PLAN AND EVALUATE WITH THE MEDIA SPECIALIST. Sometimes the media specialist either consciously or unconsciously gives the impression that this is *his* or *her* media center. The appointment of this advisory committee is one way to modify this perception, and insures that the interests and concerns of the faculty and students are considered in planning the program.

SCHEDULE THE MEDIA SPECIALIST FOR CO-CURRICULAR OR OTHER ACTIVITIES ONLY WHEN THE MEDIA PROGRAM WILL NOT BE IMPAIRED. The media specialist should share these activities but should be assigned those which do not interfere with media services responsibilities, e.g., assigned as representative to a district committee rather than bus duties during the time the media center should be open after school.

ENCOURAGE TEACHERS TO ASSIST IN THE SELECTION OF NEW MATERIALS. Some teachers will suggest new materials for purchase more readily if they know the principal favors this practice.

APPOINT THE MEDIA SPECIALIST TO SERVE ON CURRICULUM AND PLANNING COMMITTEES. Media specialists should let principals know that on these committees they can research available materials, suggest the most effective use of these materials, offer suggestions for student activities, and help set objectives and evaluation procedures.

COOPERATE IN REQUIRING STUDENT CONDUCT IN THE MEDIA CENTER WHICH IS CONDUCIVE TO READING AND STUDY. Principals are usually apt to be too strict rather than too lenient in their requirement of student behavior. A happy medium between boistrous noise and strict silence can be achieved—and a level of noise that indicates relaxed but purposeful activity.

DEMONSTRATE HIS ATTITUDE TOWARD THE MEDIA CENTER BY HIS PERSONAL USE OF MATERIALS. Principals set a good example when they give teachers and students the opportunity occasionally to observe them in the media center reading a magazine or book or looking at a filmstrip, etc. Principals probably say, "Who has the time?" But those few minutes would pay big dividends.

Teachers also have certain expectations concerning the principal's role in the media program. When principals are aware of these and conscientiously strive to fulfill them, media programs are invigorated and become more potent.

FROM THE TEACHER'S POINT OF VIEW, THE PRINCIPAL SHOULD: UNDERSTAND HOW MEDIA SERVICES ARE INTEGRATED WITH THE INSTRUCTIONAL PROGRAM. This understanding has its roots in a philosophy which includes the belief that an instructional program of high quality depends upon excellent media services. This philosophy is translated into a school program wherein instruction is so fused with media services that neither stands as an isolated or even as a separate entity.

DEMONSTRATE A PHILOSOPHY OF EDUCATION WHICH PROVIDES TIME FOR STUDENTS TO USE THE MEDIA CENTER. This philosophy focuses on the user and on concern for maximum access to varied resources for learning. The principal encourages teachers to allow students to go to the media center for purposeful activity. The principal must be sure that the media center is easily available for teacher and student use for an adequate length of time before and after school. The feasibility of keeping the media center open on some nights and on Saturday is investigated.

PROVIDE TIME FOR TEACHER-MEDIA SPECIALIST PLANNING. This is so vital that the principal will explore every means to achieve it: designating time before or after school, using aides to free teachers to meet with the media specialist, urging teachers to use their unassigned periods for planning, scheduling team teachers to a common unassigned period so that the group is available to plan together and to confer with the media specialist, investigating the possibility of one-half of the school day a month for planning.

PROVIDE FOR FLEXIBLE USE OF THE MEDIA CENTER BY INDIVIDUALS AND GROUPS COMING FROM CLASSROOMS OR FROM OTHER AREAS IN THE SCHOOL. Instead of prescribing a rigid schedule the principal will expect the teacher and media specialist cooperatively to plan times for students to go to the media center as there is a need for information retrieval, reading, aural or visual activities, or browsing.

INVOLVE TEACHERS IN THE SELECTION OF NEW MATERIALS. Teachers expect to be and should be consulted about the selection of materials which their classes will use since they are familiar with student needs and the course of study. Principals should encourage this participation by teachers.

ENCOURAGE INNOVATIVE USE OF MEDIA. Most teachers enjoy devising new and more productive ways to use media when they know principals approve of this. Nothing stifles creativity more than a principal who is critical of deviation from established patterns.

INTERPRET THE MEDIA PROGRAM TO SUPERINTENDENT, TEACHERS, AND PARENTS TO ENLIST THEIR SUPPORT. The principal who defines excellent media services to the school community and interprets their vital role in independent learning not only is promoting increased use of the media center but also is building interest and support for his entire program and everything that goes on in the school.

PROMOTE CLOSE COOPERATION WITH COUNTY AND UNIVERSITY LIBRARIES. In approaching and conferring with officials of these libraries, the principal is assuming a leadership role in making available to students the best resources which are geographically within reach.

SECURE ADEQUATE MEDIA PERSONNEL. Teachers count on principals to be well-informed about the media personnel needed for the school program and to be ingenious in finding the means to secure this personnel.

SECURE FUNDS FOR MATERIALS AND EQUIPMENT FOR NEW COURSES, AND ADEQUATE CONTINUING FUNDS FOR ALL TYPES OF MEDIA. Teachers expect principals to be aware of the need for new materials as the curriculum is revised, new courses are developed, and the range of student need and ability increasingly widens. Principals also should understand the degree of attrition that is normal today in the actively used media collection and should consider the need to replace and update. Principals should confer with the superintendent on ways to increase the media allocation to meet the rising costs of print and non-print materials and the speedier obsolescence than heretofore of many materials. Teachers also look to principals to provide equipment for students and teachers to use in the production of media, sufficient filing cabinets for non-print materials and other appropriate furniture to make the media center an attracticve and functional learning facility.

INDICATE INTEREST IN SPECIAL PROJECTS. When teachers develop activities to broaden students experiences and to add zest to learning they look for the principal's enthusiastic support which very often assures success.

PROVIDE LEADERSHIP IN A PROGRAM OF PROFESSIONAL GROWTH. Teachers anticipate that principals will be active in fostering a continuing inservice education program in cooperation with teachers and media staff. The principal will be sure that needs are identified, goals and objectives set, activities planned and carried out, and assessment of progress made.

In concluding this exploration of the role of the principal this statement is emphasized: the principal should be an active promoter of the media program in the school and community. When such an overall focus is planned with the cooperation of teachers, media specialist, students, and parents, the whole school program will be vitalized and a valuable dimension will be added to the learning situation.

> BASIC RESPONSIBILITIES FOR PRINCIPALS IN THIS AREA
>
> TO KNOW AND ACCEPT THE DIMENSIONS OF THE PRINCIPAL'S KEY ROLE IN THE MEDIA PROGRAM.
>
> TO BE AWARE OF WAYS TO FULFILL THIS ROLE IN AN ADEQUATE FASHION AND TO EXTEND PROFESSIONAL EXPERTISE.
>
> TO MONITOR THE QUALITY OF THE MEDIA PROGRAM AS IT CONTRIBUTES TO THE OBJECTIVES OF THE SCHOOL PROGRAM.

SCENARIO

East Elementary School has a media specialist who believes that the media center could be more productive in establishing a better learning environmnet, in improving student attitude toward learning, and in supporting the total school program. Of the six hundred students, one hundred and thirty-five are from minority groups and most of them ride the school bus. She sees the media center as a force to unify the newly integrated facility.

Using many of her after school hours, this media specialist

outlined and developed a plan which, in her opinion, could benefit both students and teachers. The plan included the planning of special learning sequences for low achievers and for advanced students, much individual and small group work in the media center, the promotion of increased use of non-print media, continuing consultations with teachers, and the setting of objectives and periodic evaluations. The principal, when consulted about the plan, told her to initiate any measures she thought advisable.

Questions:
1. How could the principal demonstrate leadership?
2. In what ways would the principal's concept of a media center affect his approach to the plan?
3. In what ways should the principal involve others in the school community?
4. What follow-up steps should be taken?

5

WHAT IS THE ROLE OF THE TEACHER?

The principals who have a sound understanding of their responsibilities in the media program will want to understand thoroughly the roles of the two groups with whom they will interact so closely - the teachers and the members of the media staff.

For the teachers' and media staff's roles in the media program to be effective there should be a common perception of media services, a common commitment to goals, and a common understanding of the need to work together on a continuing basis.

First, we'll examine the teacher's role. Effectively functioning media services require the participation of teachers who have a positive attitude, an understanding of the impact upon learning when print and non-print materials are utilized widely by students, competency in new teaching techniques, (and willingness to learn and practice some in which they are not yet fully at home), and a desire to become involved in a team effort to effect increasingly productive learning through the use of media.

Teachers who have an understanding of the dimensions and potentials of media services are eager to arrange conferences with the media staff and are receptive to cooperative planning to revise the curriculum or to find different approaches to learning problems. Their positive attitudes cause them to welcome the opportunity to use new materials and equipment even though this might require a change of teaching methods or class organization.

Teachers have gradually learned to appreciate the availability of a variety of materials since the demise of the single textbook "lockstep" teaching method and the introduction into the classroom of library books and a bewildering array of new technology. Some teachers have learned through up-to-date training programs to use many different types of media in imaginative ways but many still need help to grasp the value of a centrally organized and managed circulating collection of media and accompanying services. This situation often occurs when the principal purchases materials for the use of classes and neglects to have them inventoried, organized, processed and circulated as needed through the media center. Some teachers then use only those instructional materials that happen to be in their class areas and overlook the wide variety of other materials in the media center. When all materials are handled as part of the media center's collection, the media specialist is informed about them and, in planning with teachers, can effectively stimulate and administer the use of those materials, whether they be physically located in the class areas or in the media center. These practices implement curriculum objectives.

As the traditional dividing line between "text" and "other" materials fade away, it is recommended that principals employ additional clerks so that basal textbooks can also be handled through the media center. It is undesirable even impossible for the media specialist to assume this supervisory responsibility without support staff. *Media Programs: District and School* supports this recommendation. "The organization, housing, distribution and inventory of instructional systems, including textbooks, is recommended as a function of the school media program. This function requires the provision of one or more media aides, as needed, working with media professionals and teachers."(27)

As teachers develop new teaching techniques they increase the number of types of media used and they incorporate the media program more extensively into their instruction. The teacher who is entrenched in the old rut of textbook-centered teaching finds no need to use additional materials. The teacher who fulfills an adequate role in the media program is one who is eager to originate innovative instructional methods to find ways of making learning more tailored to individuals, more interesting and more exciting.

When teachers and the media staff have a commitment to common goals they are inclined to see eye-to-eye on objectives, instructional materials, learning activities, and evaluation. They will have a rapport, an understanding of each other's problems, and an empathy with each others successes and failures. The principal will want to encourage the participation of the staff in the development of the school goals, to clarify where there is misunderstanding, and to hold to these goals for underlying guidance in all activities. When the principal demonstrates command of this responsibility, the teachers and media specialist will be likely to feel committed to a common purpose.

The need for teachers and the media staff to work together is daily becoming more apparent. A team effort has always been productive but it now becomes a necessity as the single-textbook method of instruction becomes increasingly unusable and since many of the glossy media packages have been proved to be fortunately neither so "teacher proof" nor so successful as they were ballyhooed to be! As a result, instructional methods must be modified and skills in the use of materials and operation of equipment must be perfected. One of the media specialist's duties is to keep informed about new formats, new methods, new materials and new equipment, not expecting to replace but to reinforce what is already in use. Teachers and media specialist working together can devise and perfect new techniques for individual and group needs to make learning more diversified, more satisfying, and more effective.

This need for consultation with the media specialist is only one of several teacher needs which characterize the teacher's role in the media program. These needs are listed by Prostano and Prostano.(32)

> "A need for curriculum development assistance.
> A need for cooperating teacher specialists. Team teaching may be structured to include the media specialist.
> A need to create and modify media related to the improvement of instruction.
> A need for production services, specifically in the reproduction and duplication of media.
> A need to improve knowledge and skills in order to operate effectively in an extensive media approach to learning.
> A need for information about media, service, utilization, students.

A need for assistance in the selection of media to be used in teaching and learning.

A need for interaction with media, students, associates, and library media specialists on a continuing basis.

A need for assurance that their expectations for students are being met.

A need for opportunity to be creative and effective in their work."

As the teacher seeks to fill these needs he or she plays an increasingly prominent role in he media program. The principal promotes this role by requiring the teacher to:

PROMOTE CONTINUOUS, PURPOSEFUL USE OF THE MEDIA CENTER.

The primary goal is not simply to send students to the media center but rather to help students learn more effectively. The principal encourages teachers to make use of all materials available in the class area, the media center, and the community. Teachers permit students to go to the media center after giving them guidance as to the specific purposes of using relevant media.

DEMONSTRATE AN ACTIVE INTEREST IN DEVELOPING THE MATERIALS COLLECTION IN HIS OR HER SUBJECT AREA.

Some teachers may complain that there's nothing in the media center which is useful for their classes. The answer to this is diligent work with the media specialist to locate needed materials and to have them ordered. There *are* materials related to almost every subject under the sun! Many teachers take pride in the fine collections for their classes which they have helped develop in the media center.

BE KNOWLEDGABLE ABOUT MEDIA CENTER RESOURCES IN HIS OR HER SUBJECT AREA.

Many excellent media sit unused in the media center because teachers are not aware that they're there. The principal expects both media specialists and teachers to assume the responsibility for correcting this situation.

PLAN ACTIVITIES TO DEVELOP A READING HABIT AND TO RAISE THE LEVEL OF READING TASTES.

Here is where the teacher and media specialist can especially complement each other's efforts. Teachers can give the media specialist specific information about each child's reading interests, and levels and the media specialist can contribute knowledge about appropriate books. Together they can plan motivational activites which appeal to students.

PLAN TEACHING STRATEGIES FOR VARYING ABILITY LEVELS AND LEARNING STYLES.

Here again teacher-media specialist cooperation pays big dividends. The teacher can work with some groups in the class area while the media specialist works with others in the media center. The media specialist can contribute suggestions based on observing and working with students so that learning patterns and media preferences can be identified and instructional plans made.

RECOGNIZE AND IDENTIFY THE NEED FOR STUDENT INSTRUCTION IN MEDIA SKILLS AND TEACH WHERE COMPETENT.

The principal expects the teachers and the media staff to be equally concerned that students acquire the necessary media skills. Skills should be taught as the need arises during the instructional program by either teachers or media specialist. They confer about the skills which can be applied as students use media sources. They arrive at decisions about levels of instruction for various groups and suitable materials.

SERVE AS APPOINTED ON A FACULTY—STUDENT—PARENT ADVISORY COMMITTEE TO SHARE THE RESPONSIBILITY OF EVALUATING THE MEDIA CENTER PRACTICES AND PROGRAM AND MAKING SUGGESTIONS FOR IMPROVEMENT.

This advisory committee can assist in offering suggestions and giving an informal evaluation of administration and services as well as helping plan a formal structure of evaluation. The principal should expect teachers to give serious attention to this service and to make a worthwhile contribution.

MAKE USE OF THE MEDIA SPECIALIST'S SERVICES IN PLANNING CLASS ACTIVITIES AND IN DESIGNING AND PRODUCING INSTRUCTIONAL UNITS.

Teachers individually or meeting in groups can use the media specialist's suggestions and they can plan together for instruction of varying time periods. Also useful is assistance in the construction of learning activity centers and learning packages.

ENCOURAGE THE PURSUIT OF INDIVIDUAL INTERESTS.

Teachers who really work at helping students to cultivate interests greatly enrich the school years and start students on the development of vocational and leisure time activities. Where there is good media access these interests inevitably lead to the use of media and for many students this is the beginning of a life-long habit of using media resources.

BE INFORMED ABOUT THE OPERATION OF A-V EQUIPMENT.

Though students learn the operation of this equipment quite easily, the teacher should be able to feel competent and secure in this area. The media specialist can instruct and help the teacher to increase her familiarity with equipment.

USE MANY TYPES OF MATERIALS AND SELECT THE TYPE BEST SUITED FOR A PARTICULAR PURPOSE.

A teacher is hopelessly out-dated if she feels that she's done her duty when she uses three or four films a year or takes her class occasionally to see a film which another teacher has secured. Groups of students in a class could be studying different aspects of a general topic and be using at various times six or seven different types of materials. One student might learn better from a film-strip, another from a magazine article. One might find a book most interesting, another a tape recording. Teachers should feel able to use materials in any format which offer learning possibilities.

PROMOTE HIS OR HER OWN GROWTH IN THE SKILL OF GUIDING STUDENTS IN THE USE OF MEDIA.

Teachers who send students to the media center and say to the media specialist, "Teach them the skills they need," are missing opportunities to work with the media specialist and to upgrade their own personal skills. Orientation sessions for new teachers are often held in the media center, and teachers may also request individual instruction.

PLAN A FLEXIBLE USE OF THE MEDIA CENTER BY THE WHOLE CLASS, INDIVIDUALS, AND SMALL GROUPS.

Teachers should plan for students to go to the media center whenever an instructional purpose will be served. Usually the media specialist posts a blank schedule for those teachers to sign who wish to bring a whole class. The number who can sign for the same period depends upon the size of the media center. Some space must be left for small groups and individuals coming from other class areas. The principal lets teachers know that he approves this flexible use.

COOPERATE WITH THE MEDIA SPECIALIST TO MAINTAIN THE DESIRED STANDARD OF STUDENT BEHAVIOR IN THE MEDIA CENTER.

Teachers would do well to be guided by the media specialist on the discipline in the media center. It is wise for all to adhere to the same standard. Students should feel free to move around quietly to locate materials. Quiet talk is also allowed. The principal supports a uniform standard of behavior.

PARTICIPATE IN THE SELECTION OF NEW MEDIA.

Teachers should make suggestions often concerning new media, should visit exhibits of media, and should read reviews in professsional publications. They should seize every opportunity to examine media in their fields. The media specialist needs their expertise in evaluating media for usefulness in their instruction.

SEEK THE MEDIA SPECIALIST'S AID IN THE PRODUCTION OF MATERIALS AND MULTIMEDIA PRESENTATIONS.

Production skills are useful not only so that the teacher can construct teaching materials but also for teaching students to produce materials. Nothing arouses interest in learning as much as guiding a student in making a transparency, a sound-slide sequence, an 8mm film. This intrigues the slow-learning student and challenges the gifted.

Teachers who have fully participated in an expanded media program could not imagine teaching without such a dimension of instruction. Those who have not been so involved, given the opportunity, are not only depriving themselves of professional assistance and support, but also are depriving their students of richer, mind-expanding opportunities.

BASIC RESPONSIBILITIES OF THE PRINCIPAL IN THIS AREA:
TO HELP TEACHERS DEVELOP AN UNDERSTANDING OF THE POTENTIAL OF AN EXCELLENT MEDIA PROGRAM.
TO MONITOR THE USE OF MEDIA CENTER RESOURCES AND TO GUIDE THE DEVELOPMENT OF INSTRUCTIONAL TECHNIQUES WHICH FULLY UTILIZE THESE RESOURCES.
TO PROVIDE WAYS FOR TEACHERS TO BECOME KNOWLEDGABLE ABOUT THE MEDIA COLLECTION AND MEDIA SERVICES.
TO EXPECT CONTINUING PLANNING BETWEEN TEACHERS AND MEDIA SPECIALIST.

The school staff for the summer program has one requirement - a day of staff development in the media center. As is usual, the requirement of in-service brings some negative remarks. The following reflects a recent occurrence in a school with 2,000 students and approximately 70 professional staff members.

Teacher A: (8 a.m., waiting for the general session)
Another of those worthless experiences. It's already hot and I'm so tired. The year has been a drain.

Teacher B: It is hard to start a summer program so soon after the close of school. But, I needed to work so I'm glad to be here.

Principal (Having presented the overview of the program he continues with . . .) We will have a break and assemble in the media center downstairs. In small groups you'll have the opportunity to talk with the media specialist and become aware of the wide variety of media services available to you. While a small group is working with the specialist, others will be involved in the variety of learning centers which have been developed and are displayed. There is an organizational plan at the circulation desk and the number on your name tag places you in a group. Use your time to learn as much about the supporting materials as possible.

Teacher A: Can you believe they are paying for this?

Teacher B: Do you use the media center often during the school year?

Teacher A: I rarely have used it in the eleven years I've been here.

Teacher B: I think you're in for a pleasant surprise. I use the center frequently and I have been able to enrich my program as a result. The services have really been expanded.

Teacher A: I doubt if it'll make any difference to me. (End of day. Waiting to begin the last general session.)

Teacher B: Well, do you think the day was wasted?

Teacher A:s *Well, guess I have some thinking to do! Even though I knew about the media center, I had no idea of how* well equipped it was and how much help could be secured. I guess I have really neglected a very rich resource. I know next year they'll have one more regular customer. You would have won a bet had we made one!

Questions:
1. What are the most necessary and really apparent factors with which the principal deals in order to have a media center which is fully utilized?
2. Consider the various ways in which teachers may become aware of and involved in the use of the media center. Outline your findings.
3. What services seem to be most desired by classroom teachers? If these services are not available, what are some ways in which they may be secured?
4. How might the planning between the teacher and the media specialist have improved the situation?

6

WHAT IS THE ROLE
OF THE MEDIA SPECIALIST?

Many elements of the role of the media specialist can be deduced from examining closely the roles of the principal and the teacher as previously described. Two additional facets are the administrative duties and the relationship with other users of the media center, most importantly, the student. All components of the role will be discussed here.

The following suggestions, addressed to media specialists, and the media staff, detail their roles in terms of communication with the principal and others in the school community.

PERSONAL CONSIDERATIONS:

Be thoroughly familiar with the school goals and curriculum.

Formulate objectives for the media program that implement these school goals.

Read and re-read the 1975 *Media Programs, District and School*.(27)

Be alert and receptive to new ideas in media center procedures and activities.

Always be accessible to teachers and students.

Cultivate a friendly, welcoming, interested attitude toward all members of the school community.

Resolve to streamline or eliminate time-consuming and non-essential routines.

Keep all collections of materials well organized for easy access.

Keep up-to-date on recent general educational trends and concerns.

COMMUNICATION WITH THE PRINCIPAL

Place in the prinicpal's hands a copy of the 1975 *Media Programs, District and School,* and discuss this with him.

Work with the principal in establishing policies and setting priorities.

Schedule a time periodically to discuss the staff, collections, facilities, objectives, evaluation and program of the media center.

Discuss the media program annual report and the budget. Place in the principal's hands each month a brief account of ways the media center has been used.

Investigate the possibility of a more flexible use of the center so that individuals and groups may come from classrooms as the need arises.

Confer concerning the possibility of appointing a faculty media committee to work with you on services, procedures and problems.

Ask to be included in any study group or curriculum revision plans.

COMMUNICATION WITH THE FACULTY

Bring the faculty into planning through the faculty media committee. Among other activities, formulate together the first steps in meeting the 1975 standards.

Work closely with chairmen of departments and inservice education planning groups.

Be alert to new media as they are developed so that these can be made accessible to teachers in well-organized collections. Be prepared to assist teachers integrate the use of new media with that to which they are already accustomed.

Send many notes to teachers about new materials received or call attention to items of interest in your collection.

Be ready with suggestions to help teachers develop new techniques as they move from the use of the single textbook to multiple materials.

Encourage faculty participation in the selection of print and non-print materials. Provide guidance on the integrated use of these media.

Keep in close touch with the counselors so that contributions may be made to the guidance program.

Supply the materials and assist teachers with the production of media.

Advertise services for exceptional students:

Reading, viewing, and listening guidance, selection of books, etc. Individual conferences for some students are often helpful.

Plan informal teas in the media center for teachers and display new materials.

Call to the attention of teachers pertinent materials appearing in professional or other periodicals.

Maintain a collection of professional material which have been purchased or borrowed from other sources.

Offer to duplicate titles much in demand. Paperback books often may be used for this purpose.

Have displays with a message for teachers at different places in the school where they will catch the eye.

Relax circulation procedures to fit the needs. Lend reference books in classrooms for a period when they are needed, and when they are not being used in the media center. Arrange for long-term loan of collections of books to classrooms. Develop procedures for loaning non-print materials for home use.

Feel responsible for keeping informed about textbooks and the bibliographies in textbooks.

Broaden the horizons of service to include many activities outside the four walls of the media center.

Visit the classrooms to give talks.

About new books

About collections of books or other media specially selected according to interests and reading levels of a class.

About the use of non-print materials.

About the critical selection of all media for specific purposes.

About the techniques of producing media.

About evaluation of periodicals.

About evaluation of television programming.

About developing personal libraries.

About critical reading, viewing, or listening.

About sources and subject headings needed by a certain class for reference work in the media center.

About the use of special reference books.

About books related to recently shown films or filmstrips.

Visit the classrooms to teach media skills, returning to the media center with the class for follow-up drill.

Visit the classroom to observe the various ways books are shared. Here is the opportunity to develop many reading interests and to improve reading tastes.

Develop workshops for teachers on the use of new equipment.

Confer with each teacher before he begins a new unit and also at intervals during the study:

Secure information concerning the abilities, needs and interests of the teacher's class.

Give the teacher an overview of available materials both in print and non-print form. Include any community resources which are relevant to the topic being studies.

Decide which of the materials would be used most effectively in the classroom under the teacher's supervision and which should be kept in the media center for student independent use.

Offer to work with the teacher in designing and developing instructional modules, such as, self-instructional packages, learning centers, etc.

Keep an up-to-date record of topics being studied in each class, either on a wall chart or in a notebook.

Keep a folder for each teacher containing bibliographies, assignment sheets, reserve books requested, hard-to-answer reference questions, etc.

Point out the strategic times when media skills may be taught.

Offer to compile needed bibliographies.

Give suggestions for effective use of various media. Describe multi-media approaches which may be used.

Assist teachers or students in preparing instructional material, such as charts, transparencies, slides, 8mm loop films, etc.

Plan with the teacher various ways in which the whole class, small groups, or individuals may use the media center.

Make a note of ways to participate in instruction.

Discuss ways to help students improve independent study-habits.

Plan for various types of student work to be displayed in the media center.

Offer to secure materials from sources outside the media center.

Indicate a willingness to participate in evaluating the suitability and adequacy of materials, student research and work habits, and media center services and facilities as they apply to this unit.

COMMUNICATION WITH STUDENTS

Provide as much individual reading, viewing, and listening guidance as possible.

Make the media center and the collections of media easily accessible.

Teach the skills of materials production.

Give all the individual help necessary to perfect student research skills.

Increase the scope of the materials collection to provide for all interest and reading levels.

Make the media center a pleasant, attractive place which draws students to its doors.

Offer suggestions for evaluating, analyzing, and organizing information drawn from many sources, including peer and community "word of mouth" information.

Encourage the use of non-print materials for research or for recreation.

Give individual or group instruction in the use of audio-visual equipment.

Help students with imaginative and creative ways to report the results of their research; giving assistance in making charts, transparencies, slides, 8mm films, etc.

Be alert to the developing problems of personality, or poor work habits, which may necessitate conferences with teachers or counselors.

Provide in all media center activities for the development of each student according to his potential, diversifying services for exceptional students.

Borrow from classrooms or outside sources, exhibits which would be of interest to students and display them with appropriate books.

Encourage student participation in the selection of materials.

See that articles about media center acitivies appear in the school newspaper.

Arrange attractive bulletin board displays and posters to stimulate students to read more widely, and use materials more extensively.

Develop among student assistants or club members (especially officers) a deep understanding and a broader knowledge of media center materials and services.

Develop a collection of games and puzzles, educational and otherwise, to attract the less academically inclined students to the media center.

Plan a listening and viewing center for independent student use of non-print materials.

Arrange stimulating discussion groups and books reviews with knowledgable visitors from the community invited to participate.

The principal probably would not be able to observe and monitor all of the above activities of the media specialist and staff. However, the principal should be aware of them and should consult such a listing as a source of suggestions which might be offered to media staff memebers to help them up-grade the media program.

Certain of these activities should be continuously monitored by the principal to assure adequate performance. One of those with the highest priority is the planning of goals and objectives of the media program and evaluation procedures with the principal and staff members. The media specialist should be responsible for the development of a sound budget to implement plans.

The general climate of the media center should also receive the scrutiny of the principal. This includes the degree of pleasant, enthusiastic service to all students and teachers, the flexibility of rules and regulation to assure the openness of the media center and ease of access, the proportion of time the media staff members spend in active involvment with students and teachers, and the maintenance of a physically attractive, inviting media center.

The principal should also expect the media specialist to involve teachers in the selection of media based on an approved media selection policy, and to work with them in curriculum planning sessions, individually and in small groups. Courses of study in the subject areas should be designed and also programs of instruction in the location and use of media. Learning contracts, packages, and activity centers should be developed, and also programs of instruction in the production of media. The principal should expect emphasis to be placed on the integrated use of all types of media. Instruction in the operation of equipment to utilize non-print materials should be planned for teachers and students.

The principal should evaluate the degree to which all media are organized efficiently and functionally. Attention should be given to the ease with which teachers and students are able to locate media. Also monitored should be the number of students who visit the media center and make use of its resources.

The principal should expect the media specialist to maintain high quality in the media purchased and to provide materials and services to implement the curriculum and to meet the needs of students with varying ability levels and learning styles.

The principal should request that the media specialist keep an inventory of all school-owned instructional materials. If basal textbooks are included, additional media aides should be employed. An accounting of the holdings of the school should be available at any time.

The media specialist's role is a demanding one. He or she is a designer, a teacher, a consultant, an evaluator, an administrator, a dispenser of services, and a practitioner of human relations. But this role has great compensations. There's no greater satisfaction than to see the success of instruction planned with a teacher or a team, to observe students gradually becoming self-directed as they use the media center to become serious learners, to watch a student's self-confidence grow as he shows the sound-slide program he recently produced, and to enjoy the development of a student's love of reading and increased interest in using other media. These examples which bring so many rewards to the media specialist and media staff could be extended on and on. Suffice it to say that this is one professional role in which there is joy in hard work.

THE BASIC RESPONSIBILITIES OF PRINCIPALS IN THIS AREA:
TO UNDERSTAND THE ROLE OF THE MEDIA SPECIALIST IN THE
MEDIA PROGRAM.
TO EVALUATE THE FULFILLMENT OF THIS ROLE IN HIS OR HER
SCHOOL.
TO ASSIST TEACHERS AND MEDIA SPECIALIST IN DEVELOPING A
COMMON UNDERSTANDING OF A GOOD MEDIA PROGRAM
AND THE IMPLICATION FOR THE TEACHING-LEARNING
PROCESS.
TO OFFER SUPPORT AND GUIDANCE TO THE MEDIA SPECIALIST
IN THE DEVELOPMENT OF A MEDIA PROGRAM WHICH IS A
VITAL COMPONENT OF THE TOTAL SCHOOL PROGRAM.

SCENARIO

Some 1,200 students are housed at East High School. Within the complexity of this organization, there exists a media specialist who is distressed. For the most part, the faculty members use the media center and take advantage of the service provided by her. Were it not for one social studies teacher, the media specialist would feel totally successful with having provided a fully functioning program to a total staff. Regardless of the efforts made, the teacher continues to reject the media center, the media specialist and the services available. The variety of attempts to confer and to provide materials are disregarded; he simply is not receptive.

Over a period of time, she reduces her efforts and finally gives up totally. Nevertheless, the concern persists but she does not want to report the situation to the principal.

Questions:
1. In what ways might the principal learn of this situation?

2. How would you approach this problem if you were the principal?
3. What are some ways in which the social studies teacher might be given the help he needs?
4. In your opinion, do you consider the media specialist is the one who needs the help?
5. If the principal should disregard the situation, what might the results be?

7

WHAT IS THE ROLE OF THE DISTRICT MEDIA DIRECTOR?

Fortunate indeed is the principal who has available a district media director to provide counsel and guidance. Different school personnel who come in contact with the school district media director have different perceptions concerning the role. Some perceive the person in this position as a leader; others as a consultant only; others as a valuable helper and champion; others as a collaborator in different activities.

No matter how the responsibilities of this position are characterized, the title in the hierarchy of school officialdom might be director, coordinator, supervisor, consultant, helper, etc. However, the perceptions of the responsibilities of this position which school personnel hold are affected very little by the designated position title. School personnel arrive at an understanding of the role as they discern their own needs and through many professional contacts experience the fulfillment of these needs. Hear what they say.

The Superintendent says, "I expect the District Media Director to be responsible on a district-wide basis for leadership in the following areas:

Working with other district personnel to set district objectives for

70

media services and to devise the means of assessing achievement of these objectives.

Interpreting standards of excellence for media services and their role in school programs to district administrative personnel and school staffs.

Consulting frequently with instructional supervisors or consultants at the district level.

Evaluating media programs on the basis of state, regional, and national standards.

Planning and justifying the district library media budget.

Coordinating the development of materials and equipment selection processes and a written materials selection policy.

Participating at the district level in curriculum revision and planning new courses, guides, original materials.

Conferring with me on:

The directors' annual report on media services, the feasibility of adopting new or untried practices and procedures, such as:

Establishing remote-access systems of information retrieval

Emphasizing the use of microforms

Participating in a network system

Organizing a district centralized cataloging center

Using a computer for purchasing materials

Installing security systems in school media centers

Using computerized learning packages

Circulating all non-print media for home use

Keeping media centers open at night and/or weekends

Cooperating with other libraries or agencies in the community on various projects.

Administering a district center for non-print and print media, i.e., a professional materials collection and a film collection.

Promoting an increasingly more effective use of school media center resources.

Participating in development of professional growth activities for district school staffs, including media staffs.

Participating in activities of professional organizations and contributing to their journals.

Promoting the use of volunteer adult helpers in the school media centers.

Assessing the quality of the school media centers' systems of delivery and retrieval of materials.

Monitoring the effective use of federal grants for media purposes.

Interpreting the media program to the community through television, radio, the press, meetings, and conferences.

Serving as a consultant to community groups and participating in community projects related to media programs.

Participating in state, regional and national media services' surveys.

Making periodic presentations to the governing Board on the status of media services in the district.

Assessing the media center quarters in the schools and suggesting changes.

Serving on school district community committees."

The Principal says, "I would like the District Media Director to serve primarily as a consultant functioning in the following ways:

Consulting with me on setting objectives for media service and in assessing progress toward goals.

Advising on the soundness of the school media budget.

Interviewing new media staff personnel and evaluating their competency.

Evaluating current media staff members as requested.

Consulting with the school staff as they plan inservice education activities.

Conferring with me on the strengths and weaknesses of the school media program in relation to state, regional and national standards.

Advising me on the remodeling of the existing media center quarters or on the planning of a new media center.

Consulting with the school staff as they select new media and equipment.

Participating as requested with the school staff in curriculum changes.

Consulting with me on problem areas in the media program.

Suggesting strategies to develop a media program which will have a vital impact on teaching and learning.

Consulting with me on securing volunteer personnel for the media center.

Advising me on the development of differentiated media staffing.

Assisting me to keep informed about the latest technology applicable to the media program."

The Media Specialist says, "I think of the District Media Director as a helper who gives me the information that I need, supports me, encourages and stimulates me by:

Being a warm, receptive, optimistic person.

Visiting me at my work periodically.

Recognizing my strengths as well as my weaknesses.

Helping me to develop any leadership qualities I may have.

Helping me to identify objectives and to assess progress.

Participating with me and other members of the school staff in solving problems.

Advising me in planning school staff development activities.

Stimulating me to develop innovative practices and projects.

Assisting me to keep informed about new materials and equipment and planning for my participation in their evaluation.

Involving me in the planning of remodeled or new media center quarters.

Advising me on the preparation of the school media budget.

Planning for my participation in developing the following on a district basis:

    Materials selection policy

    Inservice education activities for school media staffs

    Media objectives

    Written media guides

    Research projects

Encouraging me to be active in professional organizations and to contribute to their journals.

Assisting me to achieve an integrated organization and use of print and non-print media.

Devising short, simple forms for annual reports.

Assisting me to keep informed about new materials and equipment."

The District Instructional Supervisor or Consultant says, "I consider the District Media Director to be a partner in my efforts to develop the climate, the teacher competency, and the teaching resources for better learning. This partner is invaluable in:

Interpreting to me the role of media services in the total school program.

Involving me in any planning or problem-solving in my instructional area.

Participating in the development of curriculum guides.

Consulting with me on plans for teaching media skills.

Involving me in developing inservice education acitivies for the school staffs.

Fostering a cooperative evaluation and selection of new materials and equipment.

Planning for me to participate in the setting of district objectives for the media program and evaluation procedures.

Planning with me on any projected research which concerns my instructional area.

Discussing with me the annual report on the district media program and supplying me with a copy.

Conferring with me on media problems which are relevant to my instructional area."

This description of the ways the superintendent, principals, media specialists, and instructional supervisors perceive the district media director's role demonstrates that this position should be filled by a person with great versatility and exceptional interpersonal skills. With the goal of continuing improvement of the district and school programs the district media director serves as leader, consultant, helper, and collaborator to assist administrators and other school personnel achieve their purposes. Full utilization of these services offers one of the most promising potentials for progress toward educational excellence.

BASIC RESPONSIBILITIES OF THE PRINCIPAL IN THIS AREA:

TO BECOME INFORMED ABOUT THE ROLE AND RESPONSIBILITIES OF THE MEDIA DIRECTOR.

TO MAKE USE OF THE MEDIA DIRECTOR'S SERVICES WHEN NEEDED.

TO COOPERATE WITH THE MEDIA DIRECTOR ON THE IMPROVEMENT OF THE SCHOOL'S MEDIA PROGRAM.

TO CONTRIBUTE TO THE FORMULATION OF PLANS TO IMPROVE THE DISTRICT MEDIA PROGRAM.

Scenario

The principal of Glenn Middle School, Mrs. Taylor, called the media director, John Stewart, and asked if he could come to the school next Wednesday morning to advise her in a problem she was having with the media specialist and media aide. John asked that the media personnel be asked to come to Mrs. Taylor's office later the same morning.

When John arrived Mrs. Taylor briefed him on the problem. The media personnel had been having arguments and currently were no longer speaking to each other. The media specialist, Mary Ellen McNeely, had been at the school five years and had done an outstanding job organizing the media collection. Sue Ledford, the media aide, had worked at the school one year.

John asked Mrs. Taylor what steps she had taken. She said she had talked with each one and found they just didn't get along with each other and each accused the other of various things. John asked if she would send for them so that they could all discuss the problem together.

When they arrived and were seated John said, "Mary Ellen, I've known you for a long time and when you were at Trinity School for several years you never had any problems working with the staff there. What is the problem here?"

Mary Ellen replied, "The people there didn't talk about you behind your back. Sue has criticized me to the teachers saying I always leave school when the dismissal bell rings. One of the teachers who doesn't like me has been spreading that around. I've only left when my sister was sick. I didn't get permission from Mrs. Taylor because I knew she wouldn't mind."

Sue said, "I only told that when a teacher came by the media center after school and wanted Mary Ellen to help her. Anyway, Mary Ellen leaves me to help the children and teachers most of the time. She's usually working in her office. Now she won't speak to me and I don't know what she wants me to do."

"Mary Ellen," said John, "You remember how often we've discussed in our meetings of media specialists that our most important duty is working with teachers and children."

Mary Ellen protested, "I know that but I have to keep everything organized properly."

John said, "Sue can help a lot with that but you'll have to give her some direction."

"Well," replied Mary Ellen, "I'm not going to talk to anyone who criticizes me behind my back."

Sue said she was willing to try to work with Mary Ellen.

After John pointed out to both of them the necessity to maintain good working relationships they were dismissed.

John and Mrs. Taylor then discussed the situation. John summed up his impressions and indicated where each of the personnel had made mistakes. He gave Mrs. Taylor his recommendation that if they could not work well together one or the other should be moved to another position. He also said he would work with Mary Ellen on the priorities of her responsibilities.

Questions:
1. What can the principal do to improve the morale of the staff?
2. Should the principal have taken a firm stand on her expectations for the administration of the media center?
3. Should any of the teachers have been involved in the discussion?
4. What other steps should the principal take?

8

How Should the Principal Relate to the Staff of the Media Center?

The principal and media staff working together can light a fire under the media program and it in turn can renew the total school program. A prerequisite for this is the principal's understanding of the media staff members' qualifications and responsibilities.

Media Programs: District and School lists the following qualifications: "The media specialist holds a master's degree in media from a program that combines library and information science, educational communications and technology, and curriculum. . . . (Media) technicians have competencies in one or more fields such as graphics production and display, information and materials processing, photographic production, operation, and maintenance of instructional equipment, television production, and installation of system components. . . . (Media) aides have secretarial and clerical competencies. They carry out all tasks under the supervision of the professional members of the media staff."(27)

Media Programs: District and School also lists the responsibilities of media staff members. A functional description of these shows their application in the operation of a hypothetical media center.

The media specialist arrives forty-five minutes before school begins at Centerbrook Middle School. She uses the time to plan activities and materials which she had already discussed with the teachers for the small groups who will come to the media center during the day: a sixth grade group of slow learners who need further instruction on use of the card catalog; a seventh grade group who need current information on solar energy and are going to learn to operate the microfilm reader; a teacher who is going to begin work on developing a learning center on maps; a group working on a video-tape about the school program which is to be presented to the P.T.A.; a sixth grade group searching for all sources of information, including speakers, on Mexico and planning to make an 8mm film on class activities; an eighth grade group planning a trip to the local museum to study modern art; and an eighth grade group beginning a poetry unit.

In addition the media specialist needs to plan her contribution to the unit on consumerism which a seventh grade teaching team is developing. Before meeting with them during the second period the media specialist will attend a scheduled meeting with the principal to review immediate and long-range goals of the media program and to discuss an evaluation plan. She also wants to discuss with the principal a new circulation system which research has shown to be very effective. She comments on the fact that the number of retarded readers in the school has increased and asks if any money is available to purchase additional materials for them.

The media specialist will ask the media technician to work with the groups who need to learn techniques of operating an 8mm camera, the microfilm reader and the video-tape projector. She will also ask the media technician to begin preparation of a chart to use in the learning center.

The media specialist must also leave time during the day to supervise the media aide who will be receiving a shipment of new books and processing some new filmstrips. She will remind the media aide that the tape on prefixes and suffixes must be ready for the sixth grade group to hear on the wireless listening system at 11:00 a.m. Also, that by 2:00 p.m. the media aide will need to complete the typing of the criteria for evaluating television shows and the typing of a final test for a group which has been comparing the quality of two popular shows. Also needed will be a typed bibliography of poetry books suitable for the poetry group.

The media specialist knows that other groups whose work she has discussed with their teachers will be coming to the media center during the day but she already has materials on hand to work with them.

She must make time during the day for an average student who has asked for a conference to discuss suggestions for his reading program. Also, either today or tomorrow she must determine the status of the media budget and check on the media aide's bookkeeping.

The media specialist has reserved the last period in the day for working with a class which is planning a bulletin board display publicizing the use of the media center and a media newssheet. She will ask the media technician to work with the group on the lay-out and title design of the newssheet.

After school she meets with the media aide who wants to discuss problems of materials and equipment not being returned after use. She goes to check with the media technician about this but finds that he is busy repairing equipment. It's difficult to find time for this meeting with the aide because many students come to the media center before going home to find information or select a book to read or check out filmstrip viewers, tape recorders, 35mm cameras, filmstrips and recordings to use at home. The media aide is busy at the charging desk and the media specialist helps the students and also the teachers who use their after-school time for conferences.

Of course this brief description does not include all of the responsibilities of the media specialist, media aide, and media technician. However, this does give an idea of the range of their duties. (See Appendix A for complete listing of duties.) It is important for the principal to request that members of the media staff prepare job descriptions. These should be revised periodically as staff members are added or eliminated and as duties change because of modification in the media program.

The number of personnel employed for various postions depends upon the size of the school, the extent of the media program, the type of school program and the quality of media personnel and school staff. *Media Programs: District and School* recommends the following staff:(27)

> For a school enrollment of 250, 1 professional, 1 media technician, 1 media aide
> For an enrollment of 500, 1-2 professionals, 3-4 supportive personnel

For an enrollment of 1,000, 3-4 professionals, 6-8 supportive
personnel
For an enrollment of 1,500, 4-6 professionals, 8-12 supportive
personnel
For an enrollment of 2,000, 5-8 professionals, 10-16 supportive
personnel.

Some schools with an enrollment of 1,500 - 2,000, with two
especailly competent media specialists and two aides, with a
traditional school program, and with a cooperative teaching staff,
might be said to have a barely adequate media program. Another
school of similar size which has a dynamic school program which
requires extensive media services would need a much larger
media staff. The principal must be so well informed about a good
media program that he or she can analyze the situation and
determine the number of media personnel needed to implement
the goals of the school program. Requirements of state and
regional standards must also be considered. Knowing the full
range of duties will enable the principal to assess accurately the
media staff required. (See Appendix A).

Some principals have a "blind spot" concerning the need for
supportive media personnel. This usually comes from a lack of
understanding of the number of tasks involved in administering a
media center and in providing all the services. Gaver stresses that
"the importance of adding adequate non-professional staff as the
development of new services proceeds cannot be over-empha-
sized."(15) The principal must take into consideration the recently
expanded services and the addition of quantities of media in non-
print format to the media center's collection. It is almost impossible in most schools for the media specialist alone to handle
effectively both print and non-print media without additional
staff.

IN GENERAL, THE PRINCIPAL EXPECTS THE MEDIA STAFF TO:
Be responsible for the development of immediate and long-
range goals and objectives.
Demonstrate a philosophy of pleasant, enthusiastic service to
all pupils and teachers.
Maintain an attractive, comfortable media center with an
inviting atmosphere.

80

Recognize that the major portion of time should be devoted to active involvement with pupils and teachers.

Serve in the capacity of a materials expert.

Administer the media center so as to provide flexible accessibility.

Schedule materials selection and curriculum planning conferences with teachers.

Plan and develop with teachers a comprehensive program of instruction in the use of media.

Develop the media center as a true multi-media resource.

Pursue a program of keeping informed about new educational practices and new materials.

Serve on curriculum and planning committees.

Give instruction to teachers and students on the operation of audio-visual equipment.

Provide an excellent organization of materials and equipment of all types so that they are easily accessibile.

Offer service outside the walls of the media center by scheduling many visits to classrooms.

Maintain adequate budget records.

Provide materials and services for students with varying ability levels and learning styles.

Keep teachers informed concerning new materials and equipment.

Develop with a faculty-student committee a flexible set of media center rules and regulations.

Submit frequent reports to the principal on pertinent media center facts and figures.

Work with teachers on designing instructional packages, learning centers and other instructional units.

Develop a balanced materials collection which reflects the curriculum, teacher, and student needs.

Give leadership in developing a school materials selection policy.

Publicize the services of the media staff and the materials in the media center.

Cooperate in planning a developmental reading program.

Assist teachers and students in the production of instructional materials.

Maintain an inventory of all school-owned instructional materials. Evaluate media services periodically.

In selecting and employing media personnel the principal should be cognizant of the professional competencies and personal qualities required. Ward and Bacon suggest that these areas should be investigated:

"Personality

Communication skills

Selection and production of new materials

Familiarity with total school program."(42)

Questions to be asked:

Does the applicant have a warm, outgoing, flexible personality? Does he or she relate well to people?

Is the applicant enthusiastic about media services?

Are oral and written competencies in communication demonstrated?

Is the applicant adept in the selection of new materials and well-informed about all types of media?

Does the applicant know the school curriculum?

Does the applicant's past experience demonstrate leadership qualities? Skill in teaching, training or working with groups?

Does the applicant have expertise in the administration of a media center?

Is the applicant aware of the media specialist's role in the design and development of instructional materials?

The members of the media staff work with all the students and staff members in the school and must value each as an individual. The media personnel must be accepting, facilitating people who can promote good interpersonal relations. The following creed developed by the librarians in The School District of Greenville County, Greenville, South Carolina, states practices in relationships with students which exemplify many of these qualities:

1. I will spend the majority of my time working with the children and teachers rather than with "things."

2. I will make every child feel welcome in the library—even those who misbehave.

3. I will treat every child with the same courtesy as I would an adult.

4. I will gear my instruction to the individual ability level of children.

5. I will take time to talk with children about their interests and concerns.
6. I will learn as many students' names as possible and call them often by name.
7. I will remember to show students that I care about them.
8. I will try to find something to praise about children who have behavior problems.
9. I will remember that I communicate as much with my body language as I do with my oral expression.
10. I will make the library as attractive and inviting as possible.
11. I will take time to look at children when they want to talk to me.
12. I will let children see that I have a sense of humor.
13. I will find many opportunities to reinforce students' acceptable behavior instead of always reprimanding students who are misbehaving.
14. I will evaluate the rules and regulations governing the use of media and will eliminate those which inhibit access and use.
15. I will enforce the remaining rules firmly but pleasantly.

These practices may seem self-evident but they are often neglected and this disregard damages the quality of media services. Principals should ask themselves this question, "Does this applicant for the position on the media staff have the qualities which are manifested in the credo above?"

After the selection and employment of the media staff, the main concern of the principal is to establish a productive relationship—one based on mutual respect and confidence—with the head of the media center. If there is more than one professional on the staff, one should be accorded the status of head of department. In some schools the status is on a par with that of assistant principal; in others the media specialist is on the same professional level as that of the teachers. This is a manifestation of the diversity and degrees of sophistication in media and school programs.

The principal should schedule periodic conferences with the head of the media center. Some of the significant areas of consultation concerning the media program are:

Assessed needs

Since the principal has the overall view of the school program, some needs are more apparent to him or her than to the media specialist. However, the principal may not be aware of some deficiencies in media services and their use by the students and staff.

BASIC POLICIES

The principal and media specialist should discuss and agree on the basic policies of the media program to be sure they are compatible with those of the overall school program and will implement school goals and objectives.

GOALS AND OBJECTIVES—IMMEDIATE AND LONG-RANGE

The principal needs to be informed about the media program goals and objectives formulated by the school media committee and must approve these after being satisfied that they mesh with school goals and objectives.

OPERATIONAL ROUTINES - REGULATIONS, CIRCULATION OF ALL MEDIA

The principal has a responsibility to review regulations governing the use of the media center and circulation routines to ascertain whether they are too restrictive. Accessibility and the free flow of materials to students and staff can be severely limited by unnecesary rules and circulation procedures which obstruct the wide use of media.

PLANS FOR FLEXIBLE USE OF THE MEDIA CENTER

The principal and media specialist together should work out a plan which provides for use of the media center at times called for by instructional needs rather than at arbitrarily assigned times for class "visits" to the media center. Provision can be made for teachers to notify the media specialist when a class needs to work in the media center. The media specialist also needs the principal's support in encouraging teachers to let small groups and individual students go to or work in the media center. Teachers plan with the media specialist for any special attention these students need.

INSERVICE EDUCATION ACTIVITES

Principal and media specialist confer about roles and emphasize cooperative planning and relationships. Discussion also is centered on choices of content objectives, time, duration, place, materials, consultants, evaluation. Frequent use should be made of media consultants at the local and state level.

CURRICULUM PLANNING WITH STAFF MEMBERS

The media specialist might request help in arranging time to

84

plan with teachers. The principal might ask to be briefed on the media specialist's contributions to planning sessions. The principal who might not have realized that the media specialist could be productively involved in curriculum revision might become informed about the media sepcialist's role in instructional design.

MEDIA BUDGET

The media specialist should provide justification for requested increases, or for expenditures of former allotments. Also, budgets for new programs, special projects, or a revised cirriculum should be disucssed. The principal might want information on the media specialist's bookkeeping practices and might have suggestions to offer.

WAYS TO INCREASE STUDENT AND TEACHER USE OF THE MEDIA CENTER

This topic is of vital interest. Media specialist and principal both feel responsible for ensuring maximum use of a school facility which has cost thousands of dollars and which is so essential to quality instruction. The media specialist needs the principal's support in publicizing the resources widely, planning inservice activities, encouraging innovative projects and uses of media. The principal can offer suggestions to teachers and can inform the media specialist of ideas derived from observations in classrooms and media center.

MEDIA AND ACTIVITIES FOR SLOW LEARNERS, ADVANCED OR HANDICAPPED STUDENTS

The principal needs to know how the media specialist is serving these special students. He may be able to recommend materials or suitable activities. He may need to modify the schedule to provide opportunities for better media service opportunities for them.

TRENDS IN MEDIA SERIVCES AND INNOVATIVE USES OF MEDIA

The media specialist should bring the principal up-to-date on new services or new emphases. They need to assess the value of these for their school program and perhaps adopt some on a trial basis.

SPECIAL PROJECTS SUGGESTED BY MEDIA SPECIALIST

The principal who encourages experimentation and lends a sympathetic ear to excitingly different ideas will have a media program full of vim, vigor, and vitality which like a magnet will attract students and teachers.

Media specialist's annual and/or monthly reports

The principal should encourage monthly reports and make time to discuss each one with the media specialist. The principal should also review the annual report with the media specialist. Comments on the annual resumé of the media program and its evaluation would be helpful to the media specialist. Also, the principal would probably like to discuss the statistical information on the holdings of the media center.

Deficiencies in number of staff, quarters, equipment, or collections of media

The media specialst should indicate to the princpal how these deficiencies impair the media program and what additions are needed. Recommendations to be submitted to the Superintendent could be formulated if the principal has no funds for these purposes. Plans might be made to enlist the support of parents.

Student behavior problems

The principal and media specialist need to investigate all aspects of misbehavior in the media center. Discussion should center more on preventive measures rather than punishment. Teachers and students should be asked for their points of view and the principal should provide guidance for mutually agreed upon solutions.

Evaluation structure

The principal's suggestions are needed in developing evaluative instruments to measure progress toward achieving media program objectives. The principal also should set the timing for assessment so that it will not interfere with other school activities. Sometimes provision can be made to combine this evaluation with other evaluations of the school program.

There are several areas in which the media specialist has particular need of the cooperation and support of the principal:

The publicizing of media services in school and community

When the principal joins in this effort and indicates that he places a high value on excellent media services, students, staff and parents will esteem these learning resources more highly.

The selection of new media and equipment

Teachers play a vital part in this selection process yet it is difficult for many teachers to find the time to participate. Principals can remind teachers of this responsibility and indicate suitable times for this duty.

THE ASSIGNMENT OF MEDIA PERSONNEL TO EXTRA DUTIES

The media staff expects to assume a share of the extra duties but the principal should be aware that some of these duties encroach upon the time needed for media services. The least conflicting duties should be assigned to media personnel.

THE CIRCULATION OF NON-PRINT MATERIALS AND RELATED EQUIPMENT TO STUDENTS FOR HOME USE

Media specialists know the value of circulating these types of media and with the support of the principal can at least institute the practice on a trial basis. The principal who is open to new practices which have proved effective in other schools will be receptive to this.

CONTINUING EDUCATION OF THE MEDIA STAFF

Principals should encourage the formal continuing education of all staff members. Released time may be needed for staff attendance at short-term courses, workshops, professional meetings. These often are as helpful as formal, university courses.

THE CLIMATE AND OPPORTUNITY FOR INNOVATIVE ACTIVITIES

Without the interest, approval, and active advocacy of the principal when new promising ideas are proposed, the media program will probably rock along in the same old rut. The media specialist needs freedom to experiment, and assistance in implementing new plans.

STIMULATING THE INTEGRATION OF MEDIA AND SCHOOL PROGRAMS

This has been discussed previously. The point emphasized here is that without the principal's perception of this need and without his championship the media center and services can become isolated from the mainstream of the school program. The principal should promote the involvement of the media program in every facet of the school program.

In addition to working closely with the head of the media center the principal should also be alert to opening lines of communication with other media staff members. As the principal monitors media services and visits the media center and class areas, he or she will come in contact with these other staff members and can arrange conferences as required. Each staff member must feel respected and valued. The principal should foster good working relationships and cooperation. Commendations to the media staff as a whole or to individuals do much to maintain good morale.

Every principal seeks to improve learning in his or her school. The continuing communication, consultation, and planning between the media staff and the princial make significant contributions to the implementation of that goal.

> BASIC RESPONSIBILITIES OF PRINCIPALS IN THIS AREA:
> TO KNOW THE NECESSARY QUALIFICATIONS AND THE RANGE
> OF RESPONSIBILITIES OF EACH MEMBER OF THE MEDIA
> STAFF.
> TO GIVE CAREFUL CONSIDERATION TO THE SELECTION OF THE
> MEDIA STAFF.
> TO MAINTAIN CLOSE COMMUNICATION WITH THE MEDIA SPE-
> CIALIST AND STAFF.

Scenario

The principal in this middle school of 600 students has succeeded in promoting the use of non-print media. However, she needs to purchase more A-V equipment but does not have funds available. She has provided only three filmstrip projectors to be circulated from the media center among thirty teachers. One teacher whom the principal considers very competent asks the principal for a filmstrip projector to be stationed permanently in her classroom. The principal explains why the request cannot be granted at this time.

The media specialsit becomes aware that this teacher is keeping a filmstirp projector in her classroom in spite of the principal's ruling. Appeals to the teacher to return it prove useless. Other teachers complain, and finally the media specialist asks the principal for his help. The principal knows that the teacher is doing an exceptionally fine piece of work.

Questions:
1. Should the principal demand that the teacher return the film-strip projector?
2. Could the media specialist have devised other ways to get the teacher's cooperation?
3. Should the principal seek other funds to provide the filmstrip projector for this teacher even if not for all teachers?
4. How may the principal maintain good staff morale?

9

WHAT IS THE ROLE
OF THE SUPERINTENDENT?

The role of the superintendent in the functioning of the media program, as in other operational concerns of the school system, is to provide leadership, encouragement and reinforcement. Support by the official leader frequently takes the form of directives, evolved from policy, and comments presented to the principal both formally and informally. The interest and value accorded to the media program by the superintendent in word, action and general attitude can determine the degree of priority given to this program.

It is the responsibility of the superintendent to know what constitutes a good school media program and to be aware of the guidelines and standards prepared by such groups as the American Association of School Librarians and the Association of Educational Communications and Technology. He should also have some awareness of operational aspects and elements, staff requirements, sources of funds, and the type of facilities needed.

The superintendent has responsibility for working with the principals to promote good media services. This task may be accomplished in a series of system-wide administrative meetings and scheduled staff development programs.

Responsibilities of the principal are outlined by the superintendent directly or through his staff representatives. Included in his expectations may be visitations to outstanding operating media centers by principals, supervisors and media specialists, so that his leadership team can evaluate, modify and improve the local program.

The appointment by the superintendent of a well qualified district media director ensures that principals will have assistance in developing good media programs. The media director meets the expectations of the superintendent and strives to provide fully functioning media centers. This director (Consultant, Coordinator) offers help and counsel, develops inservice sessions, advises on goals, standards and facilities and encourages the use of media.

Inclusion of the media specialists on curriculum committees reinforces their importance to program development. The superintendent encourages principals to establish faculty-media services committees and to see that teachers and media staff work closely together. As is true in other areas, evaluation of the media program is stressed and the findings are used to improve weaknesses.

Numerous lists which outline the responsibilities of the superintendent are available. Writers such as Elseroad(11), Saunders(36), and Finch(13) confirm the importance of a knowledgeable leader to bring about change and direct progress. Practitioners realize the validity of such lists and respond to top leadership which directs progress through involvement and participation.

One way to highlight development of school media programs is through the annual report developed by the superintendent and presented to the school district governing body. In such a document the official leader is able to present data which reflect achievements during a given year and, at the same time, outline needs and goals. In this report there is an opportunity to note the impact of technological changes on school media collections and programs and the resulting need for more appropriately trained personnel. Also, in the annual report the need to improve existing collections and to include a strong media program in all schools may be identified.

The superintendent is the primary force in the establishment of effective media programs. By encouraging experimental programs, incorporating media emphasis into long-range planning and stressing excellence in leadership, the superintendent plays an active role in establishing quality services. The superintendent's educational philosophy is very explicitly reflected in the operation of the district's media program.

With all the responsibilities identified for the Chief officer of the School system it is likely that the individual may find it difficult to remain current in all fields. Therefore it may be wise to identify a concise source to which the superintendent can refer periodically. *Standards for School Media Programs* identifies the following responsibilities of the superintendent:(2)

1. Is informed about the school media centers' role in an effective school program and promotes the establishment of a media center in each school.
2. Works actively to improve the facilities, staff, collections, and financial support of his schools' media centers.
3. Is aware of the advantages of a unified media program which includes both print and non-print media and promotes this concept in his schools.
4. Maintains communication and works closely with school principals, media director, and school media specialists.
5. Adopts as immediate or long-range goals the meeting of state, regional, and national standards.
6. Maintains a high quality of staff in the school media centers, using parent volunteers, clerical personnel, or student assistants only in a supportive capacity.
7. Realizes that school media centers require not only adequate but excellent financial support.
8. Delegates to the media specialist, along with the principal, the careful preparation of a budget which allocates funds according to the needs of the school program.
9. Honors the advice of media supervisors, professional personnel, and the architect in planning and remodeling of media center quarters so that adequate space allotments are provided for all facets of the media program.
10. Realizes the advisability of employing a media director depending on the size of his school system and provides funds, quarters and staff for this office. Investigates the feasibility of a cooperative arrangement with a nearby school system if his school district is too small to support this full-time position.
11. Supports the adoption of procedures which ensures the widest possible use of the media specialist's professional expertise. These procedures include centralized ordering, receiving, preparation for circulation, classifying and cataloging all types of materials. Creative arrangements with other school systems for these services may be arranged.
12. Requires that media supervisors and/or media specialists be included in all curriculum planning at the local school and district level.

13. Supports the establishment of a district media center to provide materials to supplement the school media center; special collections such as films, realia, professional materials; a sample collection of commercially prepared materials; model collections of print and non-print materials; supplementary textbooks; a core collection of general reference books; and services such as the production of materials, video-taping closed circuit television productions.

This list basically summarizes all other lists which define the superintendents' responsibilities. The superintendent establishes the direction of and the attitude toward the media programs which prevail within a system. The concern for appropriate supervision, qualified personnel, comprehensive materials, and equipment, adequate budget and continuous evaluation of programs—all these orginate at the district level from the superintendent, permeate the organization, and are reflected at the operational level, the school!

BASIC RESPONSIBILITIES OF THE PRINCIPAL IN THIS AREA:
TO BE AWARE OF THE SUPERINTENDENT'S ATTITUDE TOWARD
   THE MEDIA PROGRAM.
TO BE COOPERATIVE IN PARTICIPATING IN THE FORMULATION
   OF DISTRICT MEDIA PROGRAM GOALS AND OBJECTIVES.
TO BE SUPPORTIVE IN THE IMPLEMENTATION OF THESE GOALS
   AND OBJECTIVES.

SCENARIO

September 30, 1977
MEMORANDUM
To: Superintendent
From: Director of Media Services
Re: Budget Request
   As the budget is developed, please remember the recent changes in standards as outlined in the Southern Association for Colleges and Schools. These changes require additional personnel in some of the larger elementary and middle schools.

Also, several of the schools are deficient in the number of books per student. In addition, the per pupil expenditure for library materials must be increased. With inflation, it is difficult, if not impossible, to purchase the needed filmstrips and other non-print materials.

I am available to review the specific standards and to identify the needs on a school-by-school basis.

November 3, 1977
MEMORANDUM
To:
Supervisor, Media Services
From:
Superintendent
Re:
Budget Request

I have scheduled a work session for Thursday, November 15, from 10:00 a.m. until noon. Please be prepared to outline and justify the specific needs and to prioritize them. Should this time segment not be adequate to complete the task, additional time will be made available.

Your interest in providing a well defined and fully operating media program in our schools is appreciated.

Questions:
1. Do you think the superintendent's reply to the supervisor was adequate?
2. Do you think others should have been involved? If so, who?
3. What are your recommendations to the media supervisor concerning efforts to increase the media budget?
4. What inference can you make about the superintendent's support of the media program?

PART III
OPERATION OF THE MEDIA CENTER

10

WHAT SERVICES ARE PROVIDED THROUGH THE MEDIA CENTER?

The way in which various school personnel fulfill their roles in the media program determines the extent to which curriculum goals are implemented by extensive media services focused on student needs. A strong program of media services rejuvenates a mediocre school program and continuously fuels an excellent one. The principal should be knowledgable about the range of services both current and potential. The monitoring of these services is an important aspect of leadership as conferences with the media specialist and teachers provide opportunities for the principal to make suggestions and offer guidance.

These media services include the following:

SETTING OBJECTIVES AND EVALUATING THE MEDIA PROGRAM.
> Consulting with the principal, teachers, students, and parents, the media staff develops immediate and long-range objectives and structures instruments to be used in evaluation.

CONTINUOUS COOPERATIVE PLANNING WITH OTHER STAFF MEMBERS, INDIVIDUALLY OR IN SMALL GROUPS.
> Examples: Members of the media staff
> Offer to locate an authority on snakes to talk to the class that is studying cold-blooded animals.

Discuss with a teacher a lesson on note-taking for a slow-learning small group. Develop a learning center on this.

Suggest (to a teacher of local history) that students interview elderly people in the community and record their comments on tape.

Suggest that a small group of students who have difficulty using the card catalog be sent to the media center for special help.

Offer to work with an English teacher's class on more creative ways to share their reading. Suggest that his students make a Super-8mm film on their efforts for use with other classes.

Suggest to the coach that a special shelf be set up in the media center for athletes.

Offer to give reviews of new books to the English teacher's class.

Ask her to let you work with the small group of English students who do not like to read.

Structure with a teacher some lessons on research skills to remedy the deficiencies of a small group.

Work with a curriculum planning group to research available material on an eighth grade level for a unit on atomic energy.

Work with a teaching team to plan the activities, media, and student grouping for a language arts-social studies unit on mythology.

INCREASING USE OF NONPRINT MATERIALS.

Examples: Members of the media staff

Help a student find a filmstirp as well as books on the Revolution.

Show a student how to use the microfilm reader to locate a magazine article on Lebanon.

Suggest that a student take a cassette player and a cassette on Benjamin Franklin for home use.

Show a group how to make the best use of recordings of Franklin D. Roosevelt's speeches.

Secure the equipment and set up a two-way telephone communication with an author so that the whole class may participate either by asking questions or listening.

Show a student how he can understand the amoeba and protozoa by using an 8mm loop film.

Videotape an educational television program on Charleston for use next week by a South Carolina history class.

Put a tape on vowels on the wireless listening system for a group from an English class.

Develop a learning activity center with a sound-slide program and other materials on Knights and Knighthood for a social studies class.

Suggest that a group use the opaque projector to project a chart for classroom use.

Suggest that a teacher use a cassette to record make-up work on science for a group.

Offer to secure a film on the classification of invertebrates for the biology teacher to introduce the topic to her class.

Suggest that the home economics teacher use the media center's exhibit on the manufacture of linen.

Call the social studies teacher's attention to the media center's study prints on the development of cities.

Show the group of students studying the heart the set of transparencies illustrating the heart's action.

Show a teacher the filmstrips, recordings, pamphlets, magazine articles, video tapes, microfilm and films useful for a study of Africa and indicate how these media may be best used.

Plan with a teacher to use a filmstrip on the use of the encyclopedias for a slow-learning group.

Suggest student construction of transparencies to stimulate learners of science.

Suggest to a math teacher that some groups use tapes in the media center while the teacher works with other groups in the class area.

Alert a history teacher to useful closed circuit television programs which are scheduled next month.

ASSISTING TEACHERS AND STUDENTS IN DESIGNING LEARNING PACKAGES AND DEVELOPING LEARNING CENTERS.

Examples: Members of the media staff

Help a social studies teacher develop learning packages on three different learning levels on pollution.

Help an English teacher develop the same type of learning packages on the novel.

Work with a science teacher to set up learning centers in the media center on the life cycles of three types of amphibians: frogs, salamanders, and eels.

Help an English teacher set up learning centers in her class area on outlining, notetaking, and bibliography making.

Assisting Teachers and Students in the Production of Materials.

Examples: Members of the media staff

Help a science teacher make a set of transparencies on the principles of a guided missile system.

Help an English teacher prepare transparencies illustrating the parts of speech for slow learners.

Help a teacher and a class group prepare a sound-slide presentation illustrating the total school program for a P.T.A. meeting.

Help a student group video-tape some class skits.

Instruct a student in the procedure of taping an interview with a community leader.

Help a student make an 8mm film showing environmental damage in the community.

Help students make sound-slide presentations and sets of transparencies on the books they have read.

Teaching Curriculum Related Media Skills.

Examples: Members of the media staff

Teach the use of yearbooks to a student group needing up-to-date statistics.

Teach the use of the *Reader's Guide to Periodical Literature* to a group of students studying the Middle East.

Introduce the special reference books on science to a group of students beginning science research.

Teach students, who are making an 8mm film to summarize their study of erosion, how to operate the equipment and plan the filming.

Show students making a set of transparencies on Mark Twain how to use color effectively.

Show a student how to locate the microfilm he wants of the New York Times article on the causes of World War II.

Teach a group looking for poetry on Thanksgiving how to use Granger's Index to Poetry.

Teach students studying the lives of authors how to use the special reference books on authors.

Teach students making a survey of available material on the Middle Ages how to use the card catalog and cross references.

Teach a group needing historical information how to use encyclopedias as a starting point.

Teach visual and aural skills to a class before they use a series of films.

Teach a class beginning a study of the etymology of words how to use the unabridged dictionaries.

Teach notetaking to a class beginning research in the media center.

PROVIDING SERVICES TAILORED TO THE NEEDS OF ATYPICAL STUDENTS, E.G. GIFTED, SLOW LEARNERS, HANDICAPPED, CLTURALLY DIFFERENT, AND THE "NON-USERS."

Examples: Members of the media staff

Set up learning centers.

Develop learning packages for different learning levels.

Work individually with students.

Locate a speaker to stimulate interest and set up a regular schedule of speakers.

Set up visits to places in the community.

Secure advanced materials from university or public libraries to challenge the gifted.

Provide interesting displays and exhibits.

Work with small groups who are nonreaders working below grade level, or who are disinterested in learning.

Identify volunteer parents to serve as tutors.

Train students to serve as tutors.

Arrange student visits to the local museum and attendance at community cultural events.

Provide a paperback collection which appeals to students who are reluctant readers.

EFFECIENTLY ORGANIZING AND CIRCULATING MATERIALS IN MANY DIFFERENT FORMATS WITH RELATED EQUIPMENT.

Examples: Members of the media staff

Catalog and classify all types of media.

Interfile non-print and printed materials or have all files of non-print materials easily accessible for use with printed resources.

101

Take advantage of a centralized cataloging facility either at the district or state level.

Secure either paid or volunteer media aides for non-professional duties.

Circulate all media for home use.

Structure circulation procedures to fit the needs of the users. For example, permit the student who needs a cassette for a special project to keep it longer than the regular loan period. Set up a special three-week loan period for the English teacher's students who need the materials for an in-depth study of critical reading.

MAINTAINING A RECEPTIVE ATTITUDE TOWARD NEW MEDIA AND INNOVATIVE TEACHING TECHNIQUES.

Examples: Members of the media staff

Change the regulations concerning the circulation of tape recordings to accommodate the special education teacher who is trying a new method of using tapes.

Welcome the addition of a video-tape recorder and become proficient in operating it.

Cooperate with the second grade teacher who is trying an individualized instructional method of teaching reading.

Offer to become a member of a teaching team being proposed for a seventh grade.

Alert the principal to the advantages of joining a computer network at the district level.

Keep informed and circulate information to the school staff about new media and equipment and new instructional methods.

BEING ACTIVELY INVOLVED IN ALL ASPECTS OF THE SCHOOL PROGRAM.

Examples: Members of the media staff

Help students select pieces for a club declamation contest.

Secure the local district or state media consultant for an inservice workshop for teachers.

Plan many other activities for the professional and personal growth of the school staff.

Tell the faculty sponsor of a club that you will work with the club program committee to develop programs for the year.

Work with art and music teachers to develop excellent collections of media for their students.

Secure material from the State Library for an advanced
student working on genetic manipulation in plants.

Find background material for students taking the roles of
historical characters in a play.

Help Home Economics students find material to plan furniture arrangements for a contest.

Take part in plans for a school festival observance.

Present an assembly program with students.

Set up a display on proper etiquette for a school dance.

Secure a paperback collection for the room where children
wait for the bus.

Take charge of planning and providing materials for P.T.A.
small group discussions.

Offer to help students video-tape any school activity.

Sponsor with a group of students an oral history project in the
community.

DIRECTING AND COORDINATING THE CONTRIBUTIONS OF VOLUNTEERS.

Examples: Members of the media staff

Train a group of parents in the techniques of reading stories to
young children.

Train a group of volunteers in mounting pictures and making
transparencies.

Secure volunteer parents to take a group of students to the
county museum.

Request the director of the district reading program to train a
group of volunteer tutors.

Train and supervise volunteers in filing catalog cards.

Supervise the activities of volunteers as they assist in taking
inventory.

Arrange for volunteers to teach mini-courses in their areas of
expertise.

Coordinate the activities of volunteers who are arranging a
paperback book sale for students.

IMPLEMENTING COOPERATIVE ACTIVITIES WITH COMMUNITY AGENCIES.

Examples: Members of the media staff

Plan for a workshop for school and public library staffs on
maintenance and operation of equipment used with non-
print materials.

103

Involve the museum staff in bringing exhibits useful in summer reading programs.

Plan with the teachers and the personnel from the Environmental Protection Agency for a project for a tenth grade class on air pollution.

Work out a plan with the librarian at the nearby university for advanced students to use specialized technical materials there.

With extra materials and displays stimulate interest in the scouting camping program.

Secure a speaker from the Energy Conservation Agency.

Work out a plan with the public library's young adult and children's librarians for cooperative evaluation of new media

The examples of features of the media program listed above do not even scratch the surface of possibilities. The extent and diversity of the program are limited only by the ingenuity of principal, the media staff and teachers. Working together they can help students "tune in" to learning, and to their own potential.

BASIC RESPONSIBILTIES OF PRINCIPALS IN THIS AREA:
TO UNDERSTAND THE FULL DIMENSIONS OF MEDIA SERVICES.
TO ASSESS THE ADEQUACY OF SERVICES IN THE SCHOOL.
TO STIMULATE THE DEVELOPMENT OF POTENTIALLY USEFUL SERVICES.

SCENARIO

The principal of a large high school sent the following memorandum to the media specialist:

Dear Ms. Stewart,

I recently visited a high school in another state and noted that many more students use the media center than in our school.

I would like to have a conference with you Tuesday, January 20, at 10:00 a.m. to discuss the following questions:

How do you encourage teachers to send students to the
 media center?
What services are offered?
Do students like to come to the media center?

January 15, 1977
cc: Ms. X, District Media Consultant

Questions:
1. How much of this information should the principal already
   have?
2. What approach could be used which would give insight to the
   whole problem? (Teaching methods, teacher understanding
   of the media center, student attitudes, etc.)
3. What approach could ensure the cooperation and good will of
   the media specialist?
4. What response might you expect from Ms. Stewart?

11

How Should the Media Center Be Administered?

As the principal monitors the media program in the school one of the components to be considered is the management of the media center. Practices in this area can promote or inhibit the media program. The principal needs a clear conception of an efficient, humanely administered agency which will further the goals of the school program.

Prostano and Prostano in writing about the media center state that "the term management is synonymous with administration—. It is the orchestration of diverse parts designed to create an educational climate in which students and teachers can grow."(32) Administration of the media center includes in support of conceptualization and planning, the selection of media; acquisition, organization, access and delivery systems; maintenance of equipment; budget; personnel; records and reports, use of facilities.

It is not the purpose here to provide information in detail on each of these areas such as would be needed by the professional media specialist. The principal needs only a general overview in order to assess effectively the administration of the media center.

SELECTION OF MEDIA

This area will be discussed more completely than others

because it is so basic and because it has been emphasized recently by attempts by various community groups and individuals to censor books and other materials.

The first point to be made is the necessity for each school district to adopt a materials selection policy approved by the Board of Trustees or governing body. This policy should:

Be formulated within the framework of the educational philisophy of the school district.

Apply to both print and non-print materials.

Delegate authority for selection to professional staff members.

Refer to the Library Bill of Rights (issued by the American Association of School Librarians).

State the needs and goals of students and the school program.

State the goals of the media program.

List the criteria for selection with special attention to sensitive or controversial areas.

List the selection aids most frequently used.

Recognize the right of an individual to challenge maeterials used in the school by his or her child, but not by the children of others.

Structure the procedure to be followed—always in writing—if materials are challenged. Include a copy of the complaint form to be used.

State the procedure to be followed on receipt of this complaint.

State that no child will be required to use materials which he or his parents believe are objectionable.

State the policy toward gifts of books or other materials.

An excellent statement on policy-making with regard to instructional materials is available from the American Association of School Librarians.

Materials should be selected according to the criteria stated in the adopted selection policy. It is unwise for principals to assume the responsibility of selecting and ordering materials without consultation with the media specialist or teachers. Principals may not be familiar with the holdings of the media center and thus may unnecessarily duplicate media. Principals also may not be familiar with materials from other sources on the same subject which might be more desirable, and are unlikely to know all the teacher's needs and their students' learning levels and interests. Principals find that a few minutes conversation with a publisher's representative does not equate with careful evaluation of media. Ward and Bacon state "The first requisite (for selection) is depth of knowledge of the curriculum and the second is knowledge of the needs, interests, and abilities of the school clientele. Related factors are the amount of money available, the materials already available in the school media center and materials available from other sources."(42)

One factor which must be taken into consideration when selecting materials is the necessary replacement of titles. Books and other materials which are out-of-date or too worn to be of further use must be discarded. Principals often dislike discarding such materials either because their collection will be reduced below state or regional standards or because they consider the practice wasteful. When they stop to think about it they will realize that out-of-date materials contain incorrect information, and shabby, damaged media are distasteful to students. Principals must learn to accept discarding as a desirable way to maintain a collection of media which is of current interest and appeal to teachers and students.

The principal should expect the media specialist, school staff, and students to select materials from recognized selection aids which contain reviews by experienced professionals. Better still, those selecting materials should personally examine and review them thoroughly enough to judge their worth. The least advisable selection aid is a vendor's catalog. Though there are many fine vendors who offer excellent materials for sale, some books or non-print materials in their catalogs are better than others. If these catalogs are used, the principal should take the precaution of advising staff members to consider only those items which have an indication of favorable reviews in standard selection aids. This is usually noted by symbols in the annotations of the titles. Evidence of favorable reviews are usually not included in catalogs of curriculum materials for special programs or courses. The most reliable selection of these materials is made after examination and review. This practice becomes difficult because of lack of staff time. One answer to this is district-wide review and evaluation of materials by a volunteer group of teachers, students, and media specialists. This evaluation is usually coordinated by the district media director and could be counted for credit in an inservice education program. In some districts, released time is given for such evaluation. Some vendors will send collections of books or non-print materials to a school for review, while others will allow

108

purchase of materials "on approval" with the option of return if they are not suitable. The principal should explore different ways to ensure that materials of the highest quality are selected and that funds allocated for the purchase of materials are spent wisely. Superintendents should consider the establishment of a district center for the evaluation and selection of materials, or should cooperate with one or more other districts to provide this valuable service. Bomar, Heibreder, and Nemeyer have specified guidelines for the development of such a center.(5)

ORDERING PROCEDURES

Principals are familiar with general ordering procedures. These procedures are usually established by the school district purchasing officer or other official, and vary according to the items ordered. The items for a media center include books, magazines, newspapers, non-print materials and equipment, supplies, sets of encyclopedias, and special curriculum materials. *Media Programs: District and School* contains the following statements: "Purchase of materials from jobbers usually results in significant savings. The bid procedure is not recommended for the supply of books and related materials."(27) Bidding often results in poor service. Ordering procedures will not be discussed at great length since the principal must adhere to the required procedures in the school district. It should be noted, however, that if a principal, after working with the procedures for an appropriate period, believes with the media specialist that they have an adverse effect on the media program, he should state this, giving specifics, and suggest changes to the proper authorities. Some school districts have found it more economical and efficient to have all ordering handled at the district office, and some districts use automated methods. In any event, the principal is responsible for reviewing the media orders for correct form and attention to budgeting limits. The media specialist should monitor carefully the affects of such procedures as the frequency with which orders may be placed, the amount of paperwork, prompt or slow service on orders, and urge the principal to pass concerns on to the district purchasing officer or to the officer responsible.

The principal cannot be expected to know all the technical processes involved in organizing a media collection. It is, after all, the media specialists job to be competent in this area. However, the principal should be alert to some aspects.

Is the media specialist spending an inordinate amount of time on these processes? Sad to say, some media specialists prefer to work with things and with familiar routines rather than with people. Therefore, they unconsciously or consciously emphasize that aspect of their work. The principal should discuss this with the media specialist to ascertain the reason. It may be that a flood of new material has been ordered and there are no aides provided for the media center; if this is the case, the principal can take steps to remedy the situation. If the amount of time spent on cataloging and processing cannot be justified, the principal should remind the media specialist that the most important component of the media program is the work with students and teachers and should advise that priorities be set accordingly.

Another concern of the principal in the area of organization is that non-print materials be made as accessible to teachers and students as printed materials. Although media specialists are careful to have the book collection properly cataloged and classified, sometimes they may let the collection of filmstrips or recordings accumulate with no organization or with an inadequate one. Sometimes a year or more goes by before the principal is aware of this. If the media specialist has not learned how to handle non-print materials during his or her professional education, the principal can see to it that this lack is remedied at the earliets opportunity. In the meantime, assistance can be obtained from the district media consultant. If, by any regretable chance one is not available, help may sometimes be secured from a librarian in a nearby public library.

Another aspect of the organization of media collections which should concern the principal is whether or not to institute centralized cataloging and processing. Some vendors offer complete cataloging and processing services for the material listed in their catalogs or can supply a kit for processing these items, but then selection is limited to their materials. A few jobbers supply kits for materials listed in their own and other catalogs but the service is often slow. The lack of uniformity in these various kits presents problems in using them. Some school districts set up their own centralized cataloging centers and employ professional media specialists and aides to staff them. These centers are usually under the direction of the district media consultant or director. Some cataloging centers have used computer networks to supply bibliographic data. Principals might like to become better informed about these library networks. (See Appendix B for related bibliography). Other small school districts have worked out a contractual arrangement with another district to establish a centralized processing center that will serve two or more districts. In some states, cataloging services are offered by the State Department of Education. Cost studies have been made but the variables from school district to school district are so numerous that the results are not conclusive. (See Appendix C for related bibliography).

Principals should be aware of the situation described above and should confer with their media specialists concerning the best alternative. Gillespie and Spirt echo the conviction of most writers: "Regardless of the pattern adopted, media should arrive at the school ready for use."(16) The principal's effort should be directed toward ensuring optimum benefit from the media specialist's services in the school program. If these services are decreased due to the need to devote a large amount of time to the technical and routine duties of cataloging and processing media, it is the principal's responsibility to correct the situation. This might take the form of a recommendation to the superintendent for an increased number of media aides, or for the establishment of a centralized cataloging department if the school district is large enough to justify this.

In many schools curriculum materials for special programs may be issued from the media center but are not completely cataloged or classified. The principal should direct that this type of material be placed on the media center's inventory and be organized so that it can be located with ease.

ACCESS AND DELIVERY SYSTEMS

The principal needs to know that materials and equipment are circulated in such a way as to maintain wide and effective use. The mechanics of these procedures are the responsibility of the media

111

specialist until and unless the principal observes that too little use of the materials and/or equipment indicates that the procedures are not working. In that event, the principal confers with the media specialist and alternative plans are discussed, or the faculty-student-parent media committee might be asked for suggestions. The goal is to provide media when and where they are needed. In some affluent schools the principal may be able to purchase so much audio-visual equipment for class areas that little needs to be circulated from the media center. The principal should always be aware that certain pieces of the equipment that are in continuous use in the media center are needed there constantly and should be stationed there. Sometimes this need is not recognized.

In regard to access and delivery systems the principal should seek to implement the following:

Procedures which focus on the needs of the users.

Regulations which do not limit access to the media center during, before, and after the school day.

Flexible time periods of circulation to meet student and teacher needs.

Circulation of all media for teacher and student school and home use.

A corps of student assistants to learn about and assist in the operation of equipment.

Another trained group of student assistants to participate in the learning experiences of circulating media.

Promotion of faculty perception that teachers are accountable for making productive use of media and for cooperating with circulation practices which implement that goal.

An expectation that the media staff keep clear, accurate records of items in circulation or sent for repair.

MAINTENANCE OF EQUIPMENT

Some districts or individual schools contract for repair services with a firm in the community. Other districts maintain a center for equipment repair for all their schools. Some equipment is sent to the center for major repairs while other pieces are serviced by traveling personnel from the center. The principal should make a special effort to see that equipment is kept in good working order and that pieces are out of use as little as possible. Preventive maintenance, such as cleaning, changing lamps and fuses, and making minor repairs, is the best way to keep equipment operating. A member of the media staff usually takes care of this. In some schools the principal assigns this duty to one of the teachers, or, in very small schools, even takes on this task himself.

The principal should review and approve the media center budget. Schools may use a lump-sum budget, an expenditure budget, a Planning, Programming, Budgeting System, a line item budget, zero budgeting or performance budgeting or a combination of some of these. It is not within the scope of this publication to discuss these budget systems in detail. Principals are probably already fully familiar with them.

Media Programs: District and School states that the "annual per pupil expenditure of a school district for materials and equipment should be at least 10% of the National Per Pupil Operational Cost (PPOC)."(27) As of this date, the PPOC for 1975-76 is estimated to be $1,390. For some school districts this is a long-range goal. The following factors in preparing the media center budget are of interest to principals:

The media specialist should develop the budget after conferring with faculty members.
Budget allocations should be based on the objectives of the instructional program or special media center needs.
Each budget item should be justified.
A firm percentage for various categories of media is not desirable because of changing emphases and needs.
The principal should review and approve the budget.

The following items should be included in the budget:

Books
  New Titles
      Fiction
      Non-fiction (general)
      Reference books, including encyclopedias
  Replacements

113

Rebinding
Periodicals
Newspapers
Non-print materials (including rental of films)
Supplies (for media production, for cataloging, for circula-
    tion, for mending and repairs, for office, for publicity)
Pamphlets, bulletins

In most school districts, audio-visual equipment and other equipment, intitial collections for new schools, maintenance and delivery, and installation of special listening or viewing devices are charged to capital outlay.

PERSONNEL

This area is discussed in the section "How Should the Principal Relate to the Media Staff." Two or three considerations are mentioned here. As the principal considers the administration of the media center, attention should be given to personnel assignments. Are media aides performing duties which should be the responsibility of the media specialist? And, conversely, is the media specialist performing clerical duties which should be turned over to the aide? The principal should also notice the morale of the staff members and their ability to work together as a team. Does the Head of the media center hold staff meetings periodically to solicit suggestions for improving media services, to discuss problems, or to plan strategies? A smooth running media staff results in a smooth media center administration.

RECORDS AND REPORTS

Principals are often not aware of the number of records which are necessary in a well-managed media center. In general, they need to be sure that these records are being kept and are in order in case some specific data are needed. Gillespie and Spirt list four kinds of records: "financial, organization, service, and archival."(16)

Principals are familiar with types of financial records: budget requests, school district budget allocations, records of federal funds, or other receipts, up-to-date record of expenditures, requisitions and corresponding purchase orders, invoices, cancellations, petty cash records. Principals should inform the media specialist if they expect these records to be kept according to a certain plan.

Organization records refer in general to shelf-list and inventory data. The shelf-list is kept on cards and is a record of all materials and equipment owned, kept in the order in which they are shelved, filed, or housed. Principals may need to remind media specialists to keep this record for equipment and for collections of special curriculum materials. Records are also kept for equipment that is being repaired, books sent to the bindery, or material on short-term loan to another school.

Principals are interested in inventory records because they supply information needed for the schools' annual reports: number of books on hand and the extent of the non-print collection. Principals want to know if they have fallen below the standards of their state and/or regional accrediting organization. Taking inventory is a time-consuming process. The principal should help identify volunteer parents to assist and should encourage the training of student assistants to help the media staff. The principal should not approve the closing of the media center for inventory as this practice violate the principle of "accessibility." If the media staff is employed an extra month in addition to the regular school year, inventory may be taken during that time. If this type of employment is not practiced, the media staff can inventory a portion of the collection at various times during the year. Another alternative is to extend the inventory over a three year period and inventory a third of the collection each year. The principal should work with the staff to determine the type of inventory which would be the least disrputive of media services and the instructional program.

Service records include statistics on attendance, circulation, etc. A mindless tabulation of statistics every day is useless. Spot checks, for a specific purpose and for a limited time, aid in evaluation. To help in the evaluation of the impact of the collection on certain areas of instruction, a principal might ask for a spot check on the number of non-fiction books by category compared to fiction being borrowed. To decide whether regulations are too restrictive the principal might want a count on the number of students coming to the media center each day. Spot checks rather than daily compiling of statistics are found to be reliable. Records of equipment circulated can give the principal valuable information on the extent of the use. The keeping of all these records must not be so complicated and must not so enslave the media staff that it interferes with their work with students and teachers.

The archival records are neglected by many media specialists probably because they are not put to immediate use. Any data or materials which concern the history of the school should be accumulated and kept on file even if an orderly arrangement must wait until time can be found for this. The principal who has a pride in the school knows the value of such materials and encourages the media staff to gather and file them for future reference.

The principal informs the media specialist about the information required for reports submitted to the state department of education, to the regional accrediting organization and to other agencies as requested. Usually the media specialist is asked to include the required data in the media center annual report. This report should include not only statistical information but also the results of evaluation of progress toward meeting objectives of the media program. The strengths and weaknesses of the program should be listed along with examples of activities. Recommendations should be made for the following year and objectives stated. The principal should schedule a conference to discuss the report with the head of the media center.

The principal should expect the media specialist to submit monthly reports which describe activities in the media center, services of the media staff both within the media center or in other areas of the school, weaknesses identified, plans with teachers, problems encountered, etc. The following is a monthly report sent to the principal by one media specialist:

MEDIA CENTER REPORT
October 15, 1977

As usual, the media center opened the first full day of school, but we are disappointed that circulation has gone down some from last year. However, we still are crowded most periods and we feel students are actually working more in the media center than the previous several years. Teacher use of the media center continues to be good, and we are continually working on teachers bringing more classes and sending in more group work. Most of the students are doing individual research.

Some of our work was delayed by the collapse of some of the shelves in the new book stack forming the partition between the main reading room and the reference section, necessitating the moving of several hundred books, but this has been corrected. This partition has been very helpful, particularly when entire classes are in the media center.

Ninth grade orientation, we felt, was the most successful we have had, perhaps mainly due to more teacher cooperation. Each teacher participated in a major way, keeping the program from being basically a lecture by the staff. We do not close the media center to other students during this time, although we do have behavior problems. Some of these provide a learning experience to the ninth graders in how *not* to behave in the media center.

A meeting with all teachers new to the school was held on September 18, with all teachers present except the coaching staff as they were unable to come. However, we have talked with them individually. Refreshments were served, and the meeting was brief, but many questions were answered and the results have been excellent. This was later than usual in the school year, but we wanted to give teachers time to settle into the school routine, and we did see most of the teachers individually to talk to them about our program and philosophy and we discussed the audio-visual program during in-service.

Although it is a small group, the assistants decided to have a Media Club again this year. Several assistants are expected to join curriculum oriented clubs, but they may be associate members of the Media Club, and may participate in all activities except during the actual club period.

Following a request by Miss Stewart, guidance counselor, a display of career books has been set up in the media center, and a bibliography made for use of counselors and faculty covering not only individual careers, but books in the general subject area of careers of various types. There has been quite a bit of student interest in this display.

A gift of $25.00 to the media center was used to purchase paperbacks, as quite a few disappeared last year, and some were read so much they can no longer be repaired. We hope to have additional funds for the purchase of more books.

Mary Smith, Media Specialist

USE OF THE MEDIA CENTER

One aspect of the administration of the media center which should command the principal's close attention is the degree to which the media center is used and the quality of that use.

One of the principal's goals is that the resources of the media center and the services of the media staff make a maximum contribution to the school program. This goal is implemented or obstructed by the structure of the plan for use of the media center:

FIGURE 6

Implementation	Obstructions
As few regulations as possible	Many rules and regulations
Positively stated regulations	Negatively stated rules and regulations
Emphasis on helpful service to users	Excessive emphasis on discipline
Procedures and practices made flexible to accomodate teacher and student needs	Teachers and student must adapt to current procedures and practices
Teachers choose the times for use of the media center based on instructional needs	Each class scheduled to the media center at the same specified time each week
Students and teachers encouraged to handle materials	Excessive concern over order of materials on shelves or in files
Movement toward elimination of passes	Rigid requirements concerning passes
Toleration of talk and movement which is purposeful	Strict prohibitions on talk and movement
Promotion of before and after school use	Media center is open before and after school but no promotion of this use
Encouragement of student use, individually and in small groups, at anytime space is available.	Use usually limited to whole class use in elementary schools
Efforts made to promote access for non-users	No special effort to attract non-users

The principal also needs to observe the quality of the activities in the media center. There may be an impressive number of students in the center and others going and coming and a general

118

buzz of activity but the principal can easily discern whether students are aimlessly killing time and having a social visit or whether they are pursuing worthwhile objectives. Sometimes the principal observes assigned reference work or some personal search for information. Often students may be seen using books, magazines, recordings, filmstrips, etc. for selection purposes or for recreation. The principal may also assess the worth of media center use in conferences with teachers and media staff and in informal conversations with students.

Principals might think from the foregoing discussion that it would take all their time to monitor the administration of the media center. However, once they are informed about the features of special concern, often only a quick glance or a few minutes will supply the information they need. In the past, principals have sometimes ignored this administrative aspect and then when the media program has proved to be ineffective they have not had the relevant facts to provide the needed guidance. The principal who wants to be well informed about all school departments should certainly have a keen insight into the administration of the one department (the media center) which affects all other departments, and cuts across all areas of school activity.

BASIC RESPONSIBILITIES OF PRINCIPALS IN THIS AREA:

TO BE AWARE OF THE VARIOUS ELEMENTS OF MEDIA CENTER ADMINISTRATION.

TO ASSESS THESE ELEMENTS PERIODICALLY TO ASCERTAIN THE DEGREE TO WHICH PROCEDURES CONTRIBUTE TO GOOD OVERALL SERVICE TO THE USERS.

TO ACCEPT THE RESPONSIBILITY OF PROVIDING GUIDANCE AND TO MAKE SUGGESTIONS FOR IMPROVEMENT.

SCENARIO

The principal in an elementary school with 500 students is conscientious about supplying teachers with the materials they need. Several teachers have asked the principal to secure sixty dictionaries to circulate among the classes. On checking the status of the school budget, she finds that the amount allocated for instructional materials has been exhausted. However, there are funds left in the media center's budget. She asks the media specialist to requisition the dictionaries. The media specialist says that these funds are needed for the media center's general book collection which barely meets state and regional standards. Many books should be discarded and the increased cost of books makes it difficult to purchase accessary replacements. The media specialist also reminds the principal that sixty duplicate copies of a title cannot be counted toward the required number of books per pupil specified in the standards.

Questions:
1. Should the principal disregard the media specialist's advice?
2. Since the instructional materials funds have been depleted, how might the principal deal with teachers who made the request?
3. Should the principal become more knowledgeable about the budgetary needs of a good media program?
4. What other alternatives should the principal explore?

12

WHAT TYPE OF SCHOOL ORGANIZATION WILL INSURE OPTIMUM USE OF THE MEDIA CENTER?

Once the principal has a sound grasp of the scope of media services and an understanding of the most effective media center administrative procedures, a concurrent requisite is an enabling school organization to speed the uninterrupted flow of media services.

A bulletin, such as the following sample, reflects the philosophy and attitude of the school principal and a school organization which promote the widest possible use of the media center. Teachers take their cues from the direction charted at the administrative level. Policies are formulated with the official leader and the level of implementation by the staff reflects not only the expectations of the principal but also the degree to which the group has been involved.

THE PRINCIPAL'S BULLETIN

Wilmeyer Elementary School
Administrative Bulletin, Number 21

Having met with the instructional committee (the media specialist, one teacher from each grade level) concerning the use of the media center, I am reviewing my position and expectations with you. Please study the contents of this bulletin and be prepared to discuss it at our faculty meeting. Your input and reactions are important if we are to have a fully functioning organization.

In order for each of us to make maximum use of the media center, the following reflects the administration's position:

A. The schedule for all classes has been carefully developed in order to provide classroom teachers time to plan with the media specialist. Since we have agreed that the media center is the hub of the instructional program, the media specialist is to be included in the planning so that learning sequences tailored to specific groups may be cooperatively designed. Teachers are expected to use the time effectively.

B. Small groups, individuals, and entire classes are encouraged to use the media center. The teacher is expected to accompany her class to the media center. Maximum utlization is more nearly guaranteed when the classroom teacher and the media staff interact on a routine basis. A form will be posted on the bulletin board in the teachers' lounge each week for teachers to select times for their classes to use the media center.

C. Classroom teachers, with the assistance of the media specialist, select materials from the center to support classroom experiences, and to meet specific needs. Selection of materials will begin with the opening of school and continue throughout the year.

D. Books may be checked out by any student (K-6) who is enrolled at Wilmeyer. Children are eligible to participate beginning on the first day of the year. Since we advise and encourage parents to read daily to their children, the availability of books from the school media center for home use supports and reinforces our philosophy. The media specialist along with the classroom teacher should assist with student selections.

E. All materials and small equipment may be checked out for home use. This service begins one week after school opens, providing the time needed to stress responsible handling and procedures for checkout is sufficient.

F. Students and teachers are encouraged to use the center before and after school. The media center is also open during lunch. To stimulate maximum usage, the media staff is on duty full-time. In order to provide this uninterrupted service, the media specialist will not be assigned other duties such as bus duty, lunchroom duty, etc. Use of volunteers and paraprofessionals will provide the media specialist with appropriate breaks and lunch time.

Since most principals have never been media specialists, their experiences as classroom teachers with the use or non-use of the media center become the model frequently used. Periodic review of the literature, staff development activities and experience with staff members can modify the position of the principal.

The Wilmeyer Bulletin reflects some of the more desirable practices. One of these is the scheduled conference time for the media specialist to plan with the classroom teacher. Obviously, many contacts between these professionals occur in an informal manner; however, informal interaction does not preclude the needed scheduled formal planning time. Such a horizontal organizational structure is more likely to develop creative, active, responsible behavior. Utilization of materials, space and time, and the development of instructional components must continuously involve the media specialist if students are to benefit. In addition, such interaction may reduce personality conflicts when two or more teachers want the same materials or service at the same time.

The principal is responsible for creating the climate and flexible organization which stimulate cooperative leadership. Shared decision-making facilitates commitment; the principal serves as the model.

Some principals have considered with the media committee the idea of allowing non-print materials and equipment to be circulated for home use and have approved the practice. They have believed that the risk of damage or loss was justified in order to establish a positive attitude toward the use of all media and the media center. Easy access to media encourages involvement and induces the desire to learn.

In addition of making all media easily available, it is essential that maximum use of the center be promoted. Individuals, classes, and small groups should be encouraged to go to the media center from classrooms and other school areas at any time there is a need. Staff members would be expected to give the necessary direction and planning to ensure that the use of the media center is purposeful and rewarding.

Another point must be stressed in the effort to ensure an open media center and wide use of media. The principal should review and evaluate the current rules and regulations governing the use of the center. Do they severely limit the use? Are they too rigid? Have they built a wall around the media center which it is difficult to penetrate? Are they negatively stated? The principal should discuss with the media committee the possibility that some rules should be eliminated, modified, or rewritten.

Insights into how individual school units organize and function are reflected in the examples which follow. These are not given as utopian cases but only to illustrate some of the key ideas described above.

SOUTHWEST MIDDLE SCHOOL

Media Report
Open to students beginning the first day of school.

Closed for book checkout eight days before the last day of school.

Equipment and audiovisual materials can be checked out through the last day of school; also reference use of the media center until last day.

Full services are offered from 8:00-4:00 daily.

Library skills are taught by the media specialist on a need basis determined by the classroom teacher. This is done in the media center with small groups.

Beginning the first week of school all new students, including incoming sixth graders, are given a day long introduction to the media center and are informed about the services offered. The media specialist and the clerk conduct these information sessions.

Once each month, on a scheduled basis, the media specialist meets with the cluster teachers to plan ways the media center can be of help to academic teachers.

The media specialist is available on a need basis to each team of teachers and each individual teacher to plan activities on any day.

Students are assigned to the media center by the classroom teacher. During the media specialist-team planning sessions work is planned for the students and any special arrangements needed are set up for the student. Short or long term learning units are designed.

Learning centers are set up in the media center by the classroom teacher and/or the media specialist.

When the student needs to use a piece of audiovisual equipment a "hot" (electrified) carrel is made available.

124

A list of all materials and books in the media center is made available to the teachers and students and they are advised by the media specialist as to the comprehension and/or reading level.

Four conference rooms are available on a scheduled basis for small groups of students to work on projects, etc. Small group work in an academic area can also be done here over a period of several days and work and materials are not disturnbed.

Most of the instruction in the media center is done in groups of less than thirty students.

Audiovisual equipment is checked out by the teacher on a daily basis.

Audiovisual materials are checked out by the teacher and/or students for a set period of time.

Students may check out materials and equipment overnight.

Selected students are taught the proper way to set up and care for audiovisual equipment and materials and these students operate the equipment in the classroom.

The media specialist also operates the Instructional Television program. This includes the overall supervision of the schedule as well as taping and rebroadcasting programs on a schedule determined by the individual classroom teacher and the media specialist.

The media specialist arranges all outside calls on the conference telephone.

The media specialist is in charge of all media equipment including the care and maintenance of the equipment.

West High School

Media Report

Early in the school year a workshop was conducted for both teachers and students in the production of audiovisual materials and in the operation of equipment.

Media staff worked with teachers in scheduling ITV program for the classroom.

Orientation to media center for all freshmen was planned with the Language Arts Department.

Media staff assisted in the teaching of library skills either by going to the classroom or working with small groups in the media center.

Teachers sign with the media staff to bring entire classes or groups of students to the center.

Media staff meets with teachers during their planning periods, after school or at departmental meetings for planning activities, such as the teaching of media skills, developing instructional units, designing materials, etc.

The center is open the entire school day for student use, including the lunch hour.

Northeast Elementary School

The Northeast Elementary School media center is always open for individual and small group use. It is not necessary for students to be scheduled unless they need the direct assistance of the media specialist. Kindergarten and first grade students are scheduled into the media center for storytime once a week.

The media center is considered to be an extension of the classroom. Therefore, students come to the media center according to their own learning community's plan. Some children are allowed to come for circulation early in the morning, some communities schedule the media center as they do learning centers, some schedule reading groups during their language arts time.

During the first two weeks of school, the media specialist makes an effort to reach every child in every community with orientation. Library skills are taught in small groups as the need arises for a particular skill. The media specialist keeps a record in folders of skills and activities covered by each reading group. The names of the pupils in the group are listed and changed as the children change. Often teachers request the media specialst's assistance for instruction or follow-up in a particular skill. At other times the media specialsit sees that students need help in some area, and she talks with the teacher about that need.

An open schedule is posted every week for the media center. Teachers sign up on this schedule if the media specialist's time and planning is needed directly with this group or if the space in the media center is needed for a large group.

This type of scheduling allows the teacher and the media specialist to plan for meeting the individual needs of the students. It does require, however, more teacher-media specialist planning because teachers do not accompany their students to the media center unless the entire class comes. This planning takes the form of jointly developed learning packages, learning centers, or other instructional units. We have much more individual and small group use of the media center than large group use.

In general, the principal should organize the school in such a way that support for the media program is demonstrated and that easy communication between teachers and media staff is ensured. This communication may be blocked by rigid and restrictive scheduling of the media center access, assignment of the center as a general study area, insufficient time for teacher-media staff consultation, and no provision for center use before and after school.

The organizational structure of the school will make or break the media program. The principal's skill in fashioning the school framework will permit a careful molding and the eventual formation of an outstanding media program which will vitalize the total school program.

BASIC RESPONSIBILITIES OF THE PRINCIPAL IN THIS AREA:
TO PROVIDE MAXIMUM TEACHER AND STUDENT ACCESS TO THE MEDIA CENTER ON A FLEXIBLE BASIS DURING, BEFORE, AND AFTER THE SCHOOL DAY.
TO ORGANIZE THE SCHOOL DAY SO THAT TEACHERS AND MEDIA STAFF HAVE ADEQUATE JOINT PLANNING TIME.
TO DEVISE AN ORGANIZATIONAL FRAMEWORK THAT PROMOTES EXTENSIVE USE OF ALL MEDIA.

SCENARIO

Dear Mr. Carson,
I am concerned that Nancy, my kindergartener, has been denied the privilege of bringing home a library book. I have talked

with the media specialist and was told that five year old children can't read and aren't responsible enough to check out books. I was amazed and then I was angry.

As you may remember, we parents worked diligently to establish a library with ten books per child to meet the current regional accreditation standards. Why did we go to such efforts? Was it just to meet quantitative standards?

I feel you have deceived us and that the philosophy you sold us was just that - a selling job. You really made us believe that all children would have access to the center and to all the materials in it. If fact, you even stated that students would be able to check out some equipment and most of the materials. You certainly have modified your position.

I am planning to share my concerns with your superior and to express my opinions at the next P.T.A. meeting. Your inconsistent behavior and your incomprehensible philosophy needs to be exposed.

Sincerely,

Mrs. W. T. C.

Questions:
1. What plan of action should the principal follow?
2. How should the events of the case be explored?
3. What position should the principal take with the media center specialist?
4. How can the principal establish good rapport?

13

What Facilities and Equipment Should Be Provided for the Media Center?

Many principals have found that their plan of school organization to faciltate a superior media program is blocked by limited facilities and equipment. The general purpose to keep in mind when planning or remodeling media center facilities is to provide for centrally located, functional, comfortable, and attractive accomodations for the users of the various forms and channels of communication. Planners must remember that these users will come individually, and in small groups, as well as in class size groups and that they will use materials in different formats, in a variety of ways, and for many different purposes.

Principals are well trained in the general process of planning or remodeling school facilities. They involve the faculty, parents, students, and available consultants in the development of objectives and in the planning process. According to Gillespie and Spirt, "Experience has shown that it is vital to have the cooperation of all groups in the school setting—many designs have failed to function properly due to lack of consultation, especially at the planning stage, with those who would be using the media center facilities for work, study, or recreation."(16) As well as consulting with others in the school community, principals also read the literature on the subject and visit other new schools.

When the principal works with an architect on plans for a media center, he will want to be sure to make use of the expertise of the school media specialist. Even when the media specialist is given the opportunity to be involved, the principal must be sure that communication between architect and media specialist is sustained during the process of revision of plans. The following remarks are sometimes heard from media specialists:

"I never had a chance to verify that the changes I suggested were made."

"It was necessary to cut out some items to reduce the cost but I wasn't given the opportunity to offer suggestions as to where the cuts could be made with the least damage to the design."

"I would have liked to have given a final approval to the plans."

The principal will readily see the advantages of avoiding miscarriage in the planning process.

Another reminder to principals is that the media center facilities must be structured to implement the objectives of the total school program. Also considered should be the teaching methods and the type of school organization, e.g., self-contained classes, modular scheduling, teaching teams, etc. Principals must have the vision to provide the flexibility in the facilities that will take care of projected changes in objectives or organization. Prostano and Prostano declare that "Flexibility of design for the incorporation of innovations, present and potential, is imperative."[32] For instance, a principal might foresee future individualized or small group instruction. It would be short-sighted to have facilities designed which are suitable only for the whole class instruction that may be currently in use. Or, the principal may visualize in the future a greatly increased use of non-print materials, school closed-circuit television, dial-access system of information retrieval, or use of computers. If so, plans must include the necessary spaces, electronic outlets, sound control in certain areas, etc. To plan for future expansion and needs, it is wise to specify removable partitions and lighting and ventilation which will adapt to large or small spaces.

While principals do not need to be knowledgeable about many small details in media center planning, they are interested in being informed about three aspects: the areas needed for different purposes, the desirable space relationships of the various areas, and the equipment required.

The most functional areas and space relationships in general are as follows:

MEDIA CENTER QUARTERS IN THE SCHOOL

Overall space allotment-space for at least 15% of student body based on 40 sq. ft. per student. (This includes space needed for equipment)

Central location in school plant

Easy accessibility to all users (as open as possible, if this is compatible with the school program)

Location removed from gym, cafeteria, and auditorium

Outside access for community use

Location near television and radio studios and computer facility.

AREAS WITHIN MEDIA CENTER—SPACE RELATIONSHIPS

Circulation Area - near entrance.

In open media center - centrally located.

Administrative offices - near entrance and near circulation area - Access to general reading and study area.

Card catalog - near stacks.

Work space - near administrative offices, production area (may be combined with periodical storage area in small schools). Access to corridor.

Periodical and general storage - near periodical indexes and microfilm readers.

Media production area - access to equipment storage, also adjacent to dark room (may be combined with work area in small schools).

Equipment storage - access to production area, near carrels and small group work spaces. Access to corridor.

Professional area - access to teacher's lounge and media production area. Near reading and study area.

Small group work spaces, conference rooms, carrels - situated with provision for supervision.

Large group or class work area - Access to reading and study area.

Lounge area - situated with provision for supervision - near magazine and newspaper racks.

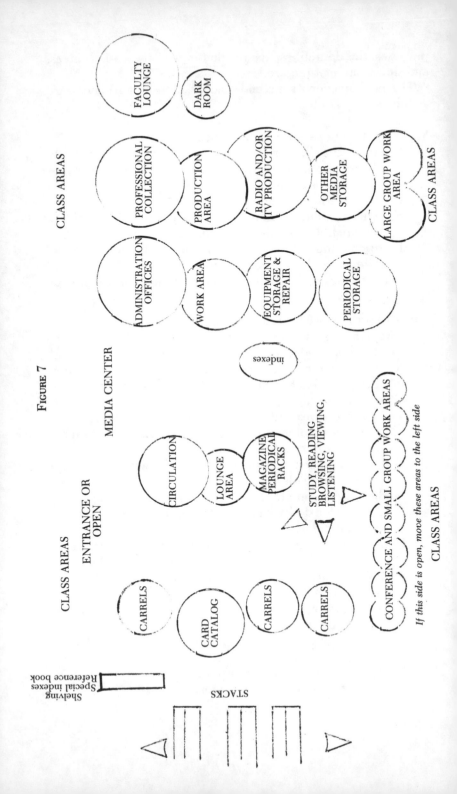

FIGURE 7

Stacks - situated with provision for supervision.

Space for special collections and displays - near entrance.

Maintenance and repair - adjacent to equipment storage (may be combined with equipment storage area).

Television and radio studios and computer facility should be located near media center.

The principal should verify the fact that the media specialist and teachers have described to the architect, or presented in written form, the ways in which the various areas are to be used and the extent of the use so that together they can arrive at proper space allotments. Also dimensions quoted in the literature may be consulted.

One possible arrangement of these areas is suggested in the plan seen in figure 7.

Principals also should know the equipment needed in the various media center areas.

CHECKLIST OF FURNITURE AND EQUIPMENT

Storage Area for A-V Materials & Equipment
Work counter
Table
Cabinet for supplies
Deep shelving, adjustable, some closed shelving
A-V equipment (as needed) - see list
Cabinet for posters

Media Production Area
Dry mounting press
Duplicating machines
Sink
Storage cupboard
Work counter
Typewriters - 1 primary
Paper cutter
Permanent wall screen
Film splicer
Copying equipment
Film editor
Stands

Lights
8mm camera
35mm camera with copy stand

Administrative Offices
Card catalog unit for shelf list (give number of drawers)
Chairs
Coat closet
Desks
Shelving
Typewriter and table
Vertical file (letter size)
Bulletin Board
Electronic Calculator

Workroom
Shelving
Sink
Storage cabinets
Typewriters
Typewriter tables and chairs
Water-resistant counter and work tables

Conference Rooms or Small Group Work Areas
Permanent wall screen
Chairs
Shelving
Table

Periodical Storage
Work counter or large table with shelving
Microfilm readers and/or reader-printer

Reading and Study Area
Paperback book racks (specify number)
Atlas case
Book shelving (5' for elementary, 6' for high school if supervision is not a problem)
Book trucks (2 or 3)
Bulletin Boards (2) (shelving under bulletin boards is desirable)
Card catalog (give number of drawers)
Chairs

Charging desk
Outside book drop
Carrels (give number)
Dictionary stand
Display cases
Informal furniture for lounge area (specify)
Magazine shelving
Newspaper racks
Index table
Tables (mixture of round and rectangular)
Vertical files (legal - give number)
Cabinets or shelving for filmstrips, recordings (tape and disc), microfiche, multi-media kits, 8mm films, transparencies if these media are not interfiled with books.

Space for Teachers' Professional Materials
Informal furniture
Magazine rack
Shelving
Tables and chairs
Bulletin board
Permanent wall screen

Large Group Work Area
Permanent wall screen
Bulletin boards
Chalkboard
Classroom furniture
Shelving

CHECKLIST FOR AUDIO-VISUAL EQUIPMENT

For those principals who are not able to purchase the optimal amount of equipment the following considerations are listed:

Filmstrip and slide projectors
The principal must decide on the basis of resources available to him or her whether to provide a number sufficient to station one in every class area plus one or two for the media center, or whether to provide an adequate number to circulate on a short term basis from the media cener.

Filmstrip viewers and slide viewers,—sound and silent
the principal must make the same decision here except that a

much larger number, at least five of each, will be needed for use in the media center.

Overhead projectors, listening centers, language masters   The principal must make the same decision for these pieces of equipment. One or two will probably be sufficient for use in the media center in addition to others in the class areas.

Microfilm equipment - 1 each, portable and stationary readers, and 1 reader-printer

16 mm projector

Super 8mm silent projector   - The number needed depends
Super 8mm sound projector   upon the number of films of
                               each type available, and the ex-
                               tent of use.

Record players   In elementary schools one for each classroom is desirable; in high schools a sufficient number to circulate from the media center.

Tape recorders—cassette and reel-to-reel   At least two reel-to-reel and five to ten cassette recorders should be assigned to the media center. If possible at least one cassette tape recorder should be assigned to each classroom.

Extra headsets
The principal can determine the number needed by consulting the media specialist.

Video tape recorder and playback equipment
Though expensive, this equipment offers excellent learning experiences and should be considered for purchase.

Television receivers
If possible one should be purchased for each teaching station and one for the media center.

Microprojectors   One for the media center, and 1 to circulate to teaching stations.

Opaque projectors   One per school is usually sufficient.

Wireless sound system   At least one in the media center. Relatively inexpensive and useful for group listening.

Media Programs: District and School contains excellent guidelines for making choices when selecting equipment.[27]

In order for principals to feel adequate and competent in serving in leadership roles in planning media center facilities they must be well informed on the basic requirements. They can then be certain that the educational programs in their schools will have the necessary resources and tools for achieving excellence in learning. A superior multimedia program integrated with the total school program is facilitated by well planned, top-notch, quarters and equipment.

BASIC RESPONSIBILITIES OF PRINCIPALS IN THIS AREA:

TO KNOW THE MEDIA CENTER AREAS AND THEIR FUNCTIONAL RELATIONSHIP TO EACH OTHER.

TO KNOW THE NEED OF AND TO PROVIDE FOR AN EXPANDING PROGRAM.

TO KNOW THE KINDS OF EQUIPMENT WHICH ARE NEEDED TO SUPPORT THE SCHOOL PROGRAM AND TO STIMULATE IM- PROVEMENT.

SCENARIO

The media specialist of North High School (enrollment 2,750) visited another high school at the request of the principal. He was impressed with various aspects of the instructional program, the organizational plan, the materials, equipment, and the school plant.

Upon his return to North, the media specialist schedules a conference with the principal and reported his findings and observations. The item that impresses the media specialist the most was the amount of audio-visual equipment available. In a summary statement about the visit, the media specialist suggested to the principal that more of the school's equipment budget be allocated for audio-visual equipment.

Questions:

1. Should the principal immediately purchase additional equipment?

2. Who should be involved in helping the principal reach a decision?
3. What factors should be investigated?
4. After action has been taken, what should be the principal's follow-up?

14

What Is the Desirable Community Involvement in the Media Program?

Historically, the impetus for the development of elementary libraries came most frequently from parents. Various organizations, such as the Parent-Teacher Assoication, gave financial support when little or none was available from the school system. Many hours of volunteered time for work in the libraries were given by parents determined to provide a stronger instructional program. Annual reports from The School District of Greenville County, Greenville, South Carolina, reflect that some 175 parents worked in sixty elementary schools to establish libraries under the direction of the library supervisor. Fund raising projects supplied resources to make the initial purchases, and parents cataloged and shelved books and typed requisitions. Currently, these same schools have full-time professional librarians and exceed the standards of the Southern Association of Colleges and Schools. The commitment and determination of the parents insured the start of fully functioning libraries in all the schools even though the budget did not include adequate appropriations.

Principals should promote the participation of parents and other members of the community in the media program. The amount of parent involvement has decreased in recent years but many parents still serve as volunteer aides in the media centers. Their tasks include shelving books, checking out books, reading to groups, assisting in the processing of new books and minor book repairs. Some of these volunteers might eventually be employed as aides by the school district.

Still other parents serve as resoruce speakers on many topics of interest. For example, in one middle school speakers from the community made presentations on the following topics within a two month period: solid wastes, the Phyllis Wheatley Center, photography, nuclear attack, careers in broadcasting, fossils, the Lewis and Clark expedition, film animation, careers in secretarial work, Russia, cryogenetics, the American Red Cross, soap box derby. It is the responsibility of the media specialist to build and maintain an up-to-date human resource file which includes the resource person's name, address, area of expertise, and availability. Stipulations for visitation to places in the community (date, time, number of participants), if appropriate for educational purposes, are also included. Being informed about the curriculum makes it possible for the media specialist to share this information with the teachers. Such sharing, encouraging and reinforcing builds good rapport between teachers and the media specialist as well as insuring the use of such valuable resources.

Teachers are becoming more active in the decision-making processes. It is all but inevitable that parents and other citizens will follow the trend. At some point in time, parents along with students, teachers and media specialists may comprise the membership of a School Media Services Committee. The varied perspectives of such a diverse group could provide wholesome direction for operating a media program. In order to be able to help community members to participate wisely a compaign must be implemented to inform them of the philosophy, goals, needs and potential of an outstanding media program. A strong public relations program is essential to generate support, both human and financial.

The principal should encourage cooperative activities with other community agencies, i.e., public library, museum, youth organizations, environmental protection agency, energy conservation groups, and higher education institutions. These activities might include joint workshops, exhibits programs, teacher inservice education, conferences, etc. The media specialist can suggest many ways of coordinating practices and services. The following might be developed with the public library: evaluation and selection of new media, summer reading programs, special non-print materials workshops, programs to reach the unserved, staff development in story telling techniques, joint skills, etc. Also, through contractual arrangements, a cooperative purchasing, cataloging and processing center might be established. Baker emphasizes the need for school media services - public library combined operations. "If the media are information carriers and if the public library and the school media program are truly in the business of management and dissemination of information, then both must be more concerned about coordinated service to meet the public need."[4]

How important the media center program is to the total school program is reflected in the attitude of the official school system leader, the superintendent. His concern and expectations are transferred to the other staff members, administrators and teachers. Parents and citizens' support of the school is in large part generated by the superintendent's leadership. Community support is reflected in many ways, not the least of which is the volunteering for a multitude of tasks. The public concepts of the importance of the media center program is reinforced by the superintendent and the numbers involved in this particular program segment are in direct proportion to the interest stimulated by his words and actions.

The principal should take his cue from the superintendent's expressed philosophy and implement it in the local school community. In the event that the superintendent does not in general encourage the involvement of community members in the school program, the principal might confer with him and get his reaction to suggestions for utilizing community resources. The principal who is committed to providing a wide range of learning opportunities for students will be able to realize this goal.

BASIC RESPONSIBILITIES OF THE PRINCIPAL IN THIS AREA:

TO RECOGNIZE THE CONTRIBUTION OF PARENTS IN THE DEVELOPMENT OF THE MEDIA PROGRAM.

TO DEMONSTRATE ACTIVE LEADERSHIP IN IDENTIFYING TO PARENTS THE STRENGTHS AND WEAKNESSES OF THE MEDIA PROGRAM.

TO INVOLVE PARENTS IN A CONTINUING STRUCTURE OF PARTICIPATION IN A DYNAMIC MEDIA PROGRAM.

141

The principal, Mr. Crumpton, and Mr. Boyle the media specialist of a high school, had developed a plan to encourage more use of
the media center. Mr. Boyle, was delighted that more students and
teachers were calling for his services. The media center was
crowded every period and the office work was piling up. Media
orders needed to be typed, a large stack of pamphlets were
waiting to be filed, filmstrips needed processing, budget information needed recording, learning packages needed typing, and
there was a backlog of books to be shelved. The media aide could
not cope with the volume of work.

Mr. Boyle conferred with Mr. Crumpton, presented the problem, and asked if another aide could be employed. The principal
said no funds were available at that time. Mr. Boyle asked about
the possibility of securing volunteer parent aides. Mr. Crumpton
was not too enthusiastic but said Mr. Boyle could try to locate
some although parents didn't seem interested in volunteering for
work in high school media centers.

Mr. Crumpton suggested using parents with special competencies as speakers. Also, he said there were places in the community
which classes could visit. He asked if Mr. Boyle had developed a
community resource file.

Mr. Boyle's reaction was negative. He said he didn't have time to
get involved in that.

Both left the conference feeling unsatisfied.

Questions:
1. What support could the principal have offered to secure volunteer aides?
2. Did the principal show a lack of understanding of the media
   specialist's problem?
3. How could the principal and media specialist have worked out a
   speakers' program and a community resource file?
4. How could the media specialist help the principal understand
   the extent of the media program?

15

How May the Media Program Be Evaluated?

Throughout public schools within the United States, efforts are being made to measure students' progress, teachers' effectiveness and administrators' competencies. In an age where there is an increased emphasis on accountability, such terms as item analysis, performance objectives, diagnostic testing and minimum competencies dominate the educational jargon. No segment of the schools' operation has been more immune to assessment then the media program. The principal should be active in directing this evaluation, along with that of all other segments which comprise the total operation, based on realistic measurable objectives. He should be familiar with a variety of instruments which might be used or modified for this purpose depending on needs.

The basic key is that the media program is part of the instructional program. Because of the organizational aspects, the principal must seek at least two different types of instruments. The first might be used to measure the quantative, logistical aspects while the second might focus on utilization of media within the various curriculum areas. Although not an easy task with which to cope, it remains, nevertheless, very important.

As school libraries evolve into instructional library-media centers, it becomes increasingly important that stress be placed on securing qualitative and quantitative as well as subjective data on the functioning of the "hub" unit in a school. Desirable elements have been identified for the unified media program, the program which incorporates those formerly designated as library, audiovisual and television. Included in these elements are personnel, facilities, resources and, finally, access to all the available learning resources. Coupled with these are involvement and commitment. Any media program, to be successful, must be understood and must be accepted.

Various assessment instruments have been designed to screen media practices and program and to determine whether standards are attained. One such instrument, *Educational Media Program Criteria* (an Assessment Instrument) has been developed by the Division of Educational Media, State Department of Public Instruction, Raleigh, North Carolina (Appendix D). This instrument includes sections on

1. Administration of the Media Program,
2. Activities and Services,
3. Personnel,
4. Physical Facilities,
5. Learning Resources and
6. Summary.

The summary reflects areas of strength, areas of weaknesses, and immediate and long-range plans for improvement. This last section provides direction for future action.

W.R. Fulton, University of Oklahoma, has developed an *Evaluative Checklist*, with revision by Kenneth L. King. This is an instrument which may be used by the media specialist to evaluate the Educational Media Program. It is a validated checklist which was developed on the assumption that a media program will facilitate the improvement of instruction. Like other elements in the total educational program, the status of the media program cannot be known unless there is systematic evaluation.

A recent (1976) evaluation instrument for school media centers is the *Purdue Self-Evaluation System for School Media Centers* (PSES) which was developed by Loertscher and Stroud.(24) PSES is actually a series of over 200 items which can be used to evaluate the services provided by a school media center. The instrument, tailor-made for a school, has been field tested in some 200 schools in the upper mid-west. Selected items from PSES could be used to measure the areas of accessibility, awareness, planning, production, evaluation, professional utilization, acquisition, and activity services. Full service is available to any school or school system for a small charge.

Liesener(23) has developed an instrument which may be used to plan a media program. It is a process oriented design that provides direction for building, reviewing or expanding media services.

An instrument which can be used for similar purposes is *The Nebraska Guide for Establishing, Developing, Evaluating School Media Programs.*(29) First published in 1973, it has now been updated. It provides procedures like Liesener's model. Careful application of the instrument provides data which results in an improved media program.

Some examples of evaluative instruments developed by the Greenville County, S.C. media consultant illustrate the informal type of instrument which media specialists can devise. One of these is *An Instrument for Self-Evaluation of Teachers and Media Specialists.* (Appendix E) After all items have been completed the scoring and evaluation may be easily established. A rating scale and interpretation of scores is included. The findings while subjective and general in nature, provide direction for improvements.

Another kind of general evaluation comes as a component of the annual report. When this report is developed, a summary evaluation is actually achieved. How effective it is is determined by the narrative which should accompany it. An example of an annual report evaluation (Appendix F) may be of interest to those who have reporting responsibilities.

Since the School District of Greenville County has almost one hundred schools the district media consultant elected to centralize evaluation of media centers and programs by having each media specialist each year administer an instrument based on the objectives for that year. Two of these have been mentioned. Others include Library Services - Survey Checklist (Appendix G), Library Evaluation by Principals (Appendix H) and *Student Evaluation of the Library Media Center* (Appendix I).

Stress on and support for the evaluation of the media program must be shared by the system administration, local school principal and media personnel. The existing program *must* be assessed and areas of strengths and weaknesses identified. Once identified, the weaknesses need to be ranked in priority order and strategies for correcting or improving them must be developed. The Media

Services Consultant should be contacted for assistance. Time lines for the completion of the activities outlined should be drawn and followed. Any plan developed should include *ways* to evaluate the results.

Evaluation is a means for determining whether a media program is adequate. It is not an inventory, although, an inventory may be basic to assessment. The narrative report which accompanies the review of the quantitative aspects actually reflects the level of implementation which the plan has achieved. The report or assessment is a validation process with a focus on impact. It speaks to the question - what impact does the media program have on instruction?

Evaluation, a continuous process, has two phases - normative and summative. The normative process is used during the developmental stages to test program objectives; its results are used to modify the program. The summative process is used with an established program to determine its success in reaching long-range goals. Both are important. Both may be used to improve the existing program.

Evaluation is a systematic procedure designed as a part of the total program. This planned, systematic function provides a way to maintain control of the goals. Any part of the total program may be evaluated. Emphasis should always be on performance; qualitative aspects of the media program should be stressed more than the quantitative factors. Starting with the objectives, instruments and techniques are sought which can be used to determine the degree to which goals have been achieved. Findings should be used to consider changes which may be needed.

Evaluation, based on objectives, is a process for determining impact. It is action-oriented; functional. It is a cooperative, ongoing process; it is essential for maintaining direction.

BASIC RESPONSIBILITIES OF PRINCIPALS IN THIS AREA:
TO PROMOTE AND MONITOR THE ASSESSMENT OF THE MEDIA PROGRAM.
TO PROVIDE SUPPORT AND OFFER DIRECTION TO THE MEDIA SPECIALIST IN THE DEVELOPMENT OF EVALUATION INSTRUMENTS.
TO PROMOTE MEDIA PROGRAM IMPROVEMENT INDICATED BY THE FINDINGS OF EVALUATIONS.

Media Specialist: I want $1000 more to purchase filmstrips and records for the media center.

Principal: You just requested $700 for the vertical file. In fact, let me check the records. Yes, just as I thought. You have used more money this year than the rest of the staff combined.

Media Specialist: The media program is the heart of the instructional program.

Principal: I have supplied the funds but you continue to fail to give the basic rationale for your seemingly unlimited need.

Media Specialist: I wouldn't ask if the need were not there!

Principal: Such general statements were acceptable at one point in time, but they are no longer adequate.

Media Specialist: What do you mean?

Principal: Does your evaluation of the media program not justify this need?

Media Specialist: You want me to help you understand the media program?

Principal: No. Not exactly. I just want to be able to justify expenditures to the public. To do so, I must be knowledgable about the needs and why they exist. In fact, I must have a thorough understanding in order to make wise decisions about priorities - even within the media program. I also want your peers to understand why so much money is being used for the media program. What difference does the media program make anyway? They need to know. They must know my position. Do you not see that my requests are actually to benefit you? Until I have the supporting data, there will be no further allocation this year.

Media Specialist: I don't really agree but . . .

Questions:

1. Why is evaluation an important aspect of the media center program?

2. Who is responsiale for making the assessment and for reporting the findings?
3. What approach could the principal have used so that the media specialist would be more receptive to evaluation.
4. What plans can the principal make to change the defensive attitude of the media specialist?

A Summary of the Principal's Responsibilities

I. The goals and objectives of the media program.

To promote the formulation of goals and objectives for the media program within the context of the school goals.

To include the media program goals in school program development.

To assume leadership in fostering the participation of staff members in implementing these goals and objectives.

II. The difference between a traditional school library and a media center.

To become aware of the substantive differences between the traditional library and the media center.

To be informed about the characteristics of an excellent media center.

To become knowledgeable about the strategies for moving from a traditional library to a media center.

III. The relationship of the media program to the school program.

To understand the interrelationship of the media program and the school program.

To be aware of how the media program and the school program can be unified.

149

To assume a leadership role in the implementation of an interrelated program.

IV. THE ROLE OF THE PRINCIPAL.

To know and accept the dimensions of the principal's key role in the media program.

To be aware of ways to fulfill this role in an adequate fashion and to extend professional expertise.

To monitor the quality of the media program as it contributes to the objectives of the school program.

V. THE ROLE OF THE TEACHER.

To help teachers develop an understanding of the potential of an excellent media program.

To monitor the use of media center resources and to guide the development of instructional techniques which fully utilize these resources.

To provide ways for teachers to become knowledgeable about the media collection and media services.

To promote continuing planning between teachers and media specialists.

VI. THE ROLE OF THE MEDIA SPECIALIST.

To understand the role of the media specialist in the media program.

To evaluate the fulfillment of this role in his of her school.

To assist teachers and media specialist in developing a common understanding of a good media program and the implication for the teaching-learning process.

To offer support and guidance to the media specialist in the development of a media program which is a vital component of the total school program

VII. THE ROLE OF THE DISTRICT MEDIA DIRECTOR.

To become informed about the role and responsibilities of the media director.

To make use of the media director's services when needed.

To cooperate with the media director on the improvement of the school's media program.

To contribute to the formulation of plans to improve the district media program.

VIII. THE PRINCIPAL'S RELATIONSHIP TO THE STAFF OF THE MEDIA CENTER.

To know the necessary qualifications and the range of responsibilities of each member of the media staff.

To give careful consideration to the selection of the media staff.

To maintain close communication with the media specialist and staff.

IX. THE ROLE OF THE SUPERINTENDENT.

To be aware of the superintendent's attitude toward the media program.

To be cooperative in participating in the formulation of district media program goals and objectives.

To be supportive in the implementation of these goals and objectives.

X. SERVICES PROVIDED THROUGH THE MEDIA CENTER.

To understand the full dimensions of media services.

To assess the adequacy of services in the school.

To stimulate the development of potentially useful services.

XI. THE ADMINISTRATION OF THE MEDIA CENTER.

To be aware of the various elements of media center administration.

To assess these periodically to ascertain the degree to which procedures contribute to good overall service to the users.

To accept the responsibility of providing guidance and to make suggestions for improvement.

XII. THE SCHOOL ORGANIZATION TO INSURE OPTIMUM USE OF THE MEDIA CENTER.

To provide maximum teacher and student access to the media center on a flexible basis during, before, and after the school day.

To organize the school day so that teachers and media staff have adequate joint planning time.

To devise an organizational framework that promotes extensive use of all media.

XIII. FACILITIES AND EQUIPMENT OF THE MEDIA CENTER.

To know the media center areas and their functional relationship to each other.

To know the need of and to provide for an expanding program.

To know the kinds of equipment which are needed to support the school program and to stimulate improvement.

XIV. THE DESIRABLE COMMUNITY INVOLVEMENT IN THE MEDIA PROGRAM.

To recognize the contribution of parents in the development of the media program.

To demonstrate active leadership in identifying to parents the strengths and weaknesses of the media program.

To involve parents in a continuing structure of participation in a dynamic media program.

XV. EVALUATION OF THE MEDIA PROGRAM.

To promote and monitor the assessment of the media program.

To provide support and offer direction to the media specialist in the development of evaluation instruments.

To promote media program improvement indicated by the findings of evaluations.

APPENDIXES

A

One Hundred Representative Media Center Tasks

The tasks have been selected from the list of 300 in the NEA Research Division's Special Report, *School Library Personnel Task Analysis Survey*. The asterisk and letter symbols in the listing for the professional staff indicate tasks that will be increasingly assumed by certain staff persons as staff size increases in response to an effective program as follows:

> * = the coordinator
> M = the media specialist
> A = the audiovisual specialist
> and in some cases a technician

Professional Staff

* Determine educational objectives of library policies.
* Plan school media programs and media center operations and maintenance.
* Help determine overall library policies.
* Assist in selecting media center staff.
* Prepare work schedules for the staff.
* Supervise work of professional and nonprofessional staffs.
* Work with and submit reports to administration.
* Determine records and statistics needed.

* Enlist faculty in writing a materials selection policy.
* Establish cataloging and classification policies.
* Plan for reorganization and relocation of collections.
* Formulate policies and procedures for circulating materials and equipment.
* Assume responsibility for decisions concerning disciplinary actions.
* Develop a handbook for teachers and for students.

M/A Schedule use of facilities.
M/A Conduct inservice work.
M/A Participate in curriculum development and review.
M/A Train student aides and volunteers.
M/A Initiate projects and activities relating to media resources.
M/A Originate and conduct special activities for interest groups.
M/A Maintain in the media center schedules of class activities.
M/A Orient students to media center schedules of class activities.
M/A Plan sequential programs of instruction in research techniques.
M/A Inform teachers of new services.
M/A Introduce teachers to bibliographic tools in subject and grade-level disciplines.
M/A Outline publicity; write articles, promotional materials, and notices for school and local papers.
M/A Work with teachers and students in reading, viewing, and listening activities.

* Work with teachers to establish procedures for group or individual assignments.
* Inform faculty of available inservice courses, workshops, professional meetings, and the community's educational resources.
* Promote use of professional library.
* Plan and participate in community relations activities.
* Visit with other schools and participate in professional meetings.
* Determine policy for accepting gifts.

M/A Plan with faculty members to coordinate materials and media activities.
M/A Observe classroom work to coordinate with media program.
M/A Participate in team-teaching and define staff arrangements.
M/A Enlist faculty participation and recommendations in evaluating or selecting materials.
M/A Develop evaluation forms.
M/A Read books, magazines, professional journals, review services, and local publications for information on selecting materials and equipment.
M/A Evaluate and select materials and equipment.
M/A Organize and maintain reserve and special media collections.
M/A Plan the system for scheduling and delivering materials and equipment.
M/A Compile media lists.
M/A Administer interlibrary loan services.
M/A Perform general reference services.

PARAPROFESSIONAL STAFF

Develop new uses for materials and equipment.
Work with teachers to design innovations in instruction.
Help to determine space for equipment to be purchased.
Develop evaluation forms.
Adapt commerical materials and equipment to meet special needs.
Design publicity materials in all media.
Make simple display devices for use in instruction.

Operate lettering and drawing devices.
Microfilm materials.
Produce specialized materials for school needs (e.g., tapes, record programs, etc.)
Handle photography and film course and recreation-related media center work.
Maintain dial-access and computer equipment and programs.
Provide for preparation of materials (e.g., laminating, making transparencies, etc.).

Make major repairs of equipment if not in contract.

Evaluate students' special media center projects.

Assist with independent study.

Assist teachers and students in using equipment and materials.

Assist teachers and students in locating and selecting materials and equipment.

Assist teachers and students with taping services.

Assist teachers and students with production techniques.

Answer ready reference questions.

Plan and prepare displays.

Plan and supervise media fairs.

Develop forms for operation of the library in area of specialization.

Maintain materials and equipment evaluation file.

Perform routine print shop activities.

Schedule use of and deliver materials and equipment.

Maintain cumulative records of condition of and maintenance work on equipment.

NONPROFESSIONAL STAFF

Determine, control, order, inventory, and maintain supplies.

Handle clerical and secretarial work of correspondence (e.g., filing, typing, mailing, etc.).

Type notices, requisitions, bulletins, media bibliographies, etc.

Assist in sale of paperback books.

Perform messenger service.

Maintain selection aids for finding new materials.

Check shelf list and other aids to prepare bibliographic data for ordering and duplicating materials.

Transact clerical business operationS: file orders and invoices; receive credit memorandum and invoices and transmit them to appropriate office; verify total purchase costs; follow up outstanding orders.

Unpack and check new materials and equipment received, and verify invoices with shipment and order.

Post receipt of periodical and newspaper issues and take care of missing items.

Make items received ready for use.

Stamp ownership mark on all materials.

Place subject headings on vertical file folders.

Adapt commercial catalog cards for local use.

Prepare and file shelf list and catalog cards.

Sort and place materials on shelves or in containers and keep them in reasonable order.

Process records for materials and equipment withdrawn from collections.

Compile and revise media book catalogs.

Compile review files for materials and equipment.

Maintain media inventory records and assist in inventory.

Set up and operate audiovisual equipment, such as projectors and videoreaders.

Inspect and make necessary repairs to print and nonprint materials and equipment.

B

LIBRARY NETWORKS: SELECTED REFERENCES

BECHNER, Joseph. Interlibrary communications and networks. (In Bibliographic Control of Non-print Media. Chicago, American Library Association, 1972, pp. 3-15).

Basic information on networks can be found here. Also discussed are the means by which data are transmitted: telephone lines, coaxial cable, microwave stations, and satellites. Included is a discussion of some of the ways libraries are using networks.

BUTLER, E. "State of the Nation in Networking." *Journal of Library Automation,* 8:200-220, September, 1975.

This is an overview at this point in time of the rapidly changing library network situation. Covered here are network definitions, the operating library networks in the country and their current status, current network resources, factors in network development, and the future of library networks.

CORBIN, John. "Library Networks". *Library Journal,* 101:203-7, January 1, 1976.

After defining the term "network," the history of networks since the turn of the century is recounted. Looking into the future, a description is given of a member library of a network in the era 1995-2015. These needs are cited: a national plan, standards, research. Future desirable cost-beneficial services are listed.

HEWITT, Joe A. "The Impact of OCLC". *American Libraries,* 7:268-76, May, 1976.

This researcher visited every charter library on the on-line system of the Ohio College Library Center system. He makes an objective report of the good and the bad.

KENNEDY, John P. "The Southeastern Library Network: A Progress Report." *Southeastern Librarian,* 23:13-15, Spring, 1973.

This article gives information about the organizational procedures which gave birth to SOLINET. The aims and purposes are listed.

KOLB, Audrey and J Morse. "Initiating School Participation in Networking" School Media Quarterly 6:52-59, Fall, 1977.

Believing that networking is of value to schools and that schools have contributions to make to networks, the authors define the types of library networks, list the factors in building a network, outline a method of appraisal of networks, and describe in detail the steps in selling the school administration on participation.

MARUYAMA, Lenor S. The MARC project and MARC records for film material. (In Bibliographic Control of Non-print Media. Chicago, American Library Association, 1972, pp. 210-213).

The Library of Congress provides cataloging information on tapes, called MARC (Machines- Readable Cataloging). This article gives basic information.

McCAULEY, Elfrieda. Computers in School Libraries. (In Ward, P.L. and Beacon, R., comp. School Media Center; a book of readings, Metuchen, New Jersey, Scarecrow, 1973, pp. 166-172).

This is a survey of the uses school libraries may make of computers including what computers will do in providing services for cooperating school districts or for several types of libraries on a regional basis.

NATIONAL COMMISSION ON LIBRARIES AND INFORMATION SCIENCE. Toward a National Program for Library and Information Services: Goals for Action. Washington, The Commission, 1975, pp. 13-16; 31-38.

This is a summary of the status of resources sharing. Existing networks are named, from local to regional. and from those embracing one type of library to those consisting of multitypes. In the school library area, a nationwide network is visualized.

NYREN, Karl. "Investing in Network Services: How Far Can We Go?" *Library Journal,* 101:1394-6, June 15, 1976.

Six librarians respond to the question of future investment in network services. Some reactions express an enthusiastic embrace of the potential of networks to improve access and to move more libraries from generalist to specialist functions. Other responses reflect a cautious concern with stretching still further the limited budgets and with needing more information on the contributions of networks.

SALIENT: "Satellite Library Information Network." *Journal of Library Automation,* 7:228-9, September, 1974.

This is a brief report on SALINET, an experiment in delivering

159

library services by satellite to sparsely settled regions in twelve Rocky Mountain and Northern plains states. Services include: public information programming at the individual level, technology dissemination and librarian inservice training.

STEVENS, Charles H. "SOLINET" *Southeastern Library*, 25:35-37, Fall, 1975.

The answers are given to three questions asked about the Southeastern Library Network:

Why do service charges change so frequently?
When can we expect to have a serials cataloging system in operation?
Will SOLINET duplicate OCLC (Ohio College Library Center) shared cataloging service?

TREZZA, Alphonse F. Networks. American Libraries Association Yearbook, Chicago, American Library Association, 1976, pp. 248-49.

Networking, "the wave of the future," is expanding at a phenomenal rate. Trezza answers these questions:

What is a network?
Who can participate?
What are the services and obligations?
What are the costs?

WELSH, William I. "Networks Explained: An Old Idea in a New Setting." *Wilson Library Bulletin*, 48:565-567, March, 1974.

Viewing networks as attempts to solve library problems that have become more and more critical, the author lists two requirements: quick communication and standardization. Also mentioned is the aim to make Library of Congress cataloging records accessible to outside users by means of computer on-line systems. How a national "dream" network would function is described.

C

CENTRALIZED CATALOGING
SELECTED REFERENCE

"BCPL Helps School: Book Processing Project." *Library Journal,*
98:689, February 15, 1973.

Brief review of a joint public library/senior high school book
processing project with a favorable prognosis.

COLE, Georgia R. "Budgeting for centralized cataloging and processing." *Hoosier School Libraries,* 11:26-29, March, 1972.

How can centralized cataloging and processing costs be determined? Cole suggests a method. A detailed budget may be
obtained by writing the author, Mrs. Georgia R. Cole, Director of
Educational Media, Vigo County Schools, Terre Haute, Indiana.

DARLING, R.L. Streamlining for Service. (In-school Activities and
the Library) Chicago, American Library Association,
1965, p. 1-2.

The focus here is on the following: centralized processing, use of
machines for processing, commercial cataloging and processing, conception among school districts; use of data processing equipment; and
printed book catalogs.

DARLING, R.L. Instructional Materials Services for Montgomery
Public Schools. (In Bibliographic Control of Non-print
Media). Chicago, American Library Association, 1972, p.
187-93.

This is a description in depth of centralized media services for a large
school district (180 schools). Special attention is given to the cataloging
and processing.

HART, Thomas L. "Centralized Processing: Gain or Base?" A study of Media Processing Center in Florida and Indiana. *School Media Quarterly*, 3:210-14, Spring, 1975.

The author concludes that "only those large centers which can produce processing and cataloging economically will survive." Guidelines and standardization for commercial cataloging and processing are needed. Centralized processing centers can be more economically provided on a national basis. Cost effectiveness studies should be made of the on-line access terminals to MARC data bases being developed by commercial firms.

D

EDUCATIONAL MEDIA PROGRAM CRITERIA*
AN ASSESSMENT INSTRUMENT

*Reprinted by permission of the Division of Educational Media, State Department of Public Instruction, Raleigh, North Carolina

Educational Media Program

Administrative Unit _____   Grades _____

Name of School _____   # of students _____

Address: _____   # of teachers _____

_____

_____

Evaluation completed by: _____, Principal

_____, Media Coordinator

_____

_____

Guiding Principles

The unified media program incorporates in one administrative structure the elements of the programs formerly designated as library, audiovisual, and television. It retains and expands the desirable elements of these programs to provide each educator and each student the contributions of a coordinated media program. The key to the media program is accessibility. This program should provide the following:

Competent personnel sufficient in number to conduct the program

Facilities designed for flexibility and convenient use

Resources of high quality and sufficient quantity to meet individual interests and needs

Access to all learning resources available

An effective media program requires the involvement, the commitment, and the cooperation of administrators, teachers, and media staff. The media program affects, and is affected by, everyone involved in the learning process. A program succeeds to the degree that those responsible for it understand, accept, and apply these principles.

Date of Indepth Survey _____

Survey Team Coordinator _____

_____

DIRECTIONS FOR USING THE ASSESSMENT INSTRUMENT

The attached evaluation forms may be completed by individuals, committees, and/or the entire faculty. Open discussion and staff involvement are important elements of successful evaluation.

Principles and criteria used in the forms follow two currently definitive publications:

Media Program Recommendations: Individual School-Administrative Unit, approved by the State Board of Education, November, 1975.

Guidelines for Media Preparation, adopted by the State Board of Education, 9/7/72.

Familiarity with these guidelines is essential. Should you require copies of the guidelines, please contact:

Division of Education Media
State Department of Public Instruction
Raleigh, North Carolina 27611

The following rating scale should be used:

5 - Excellent — exemplary practice, full utilization
4 - Good — above average practice, an adequate comprehensive program
3 - Fair — satisfactory or minimum practice
2 - Poor — unsatisfactory or below minimum practice
1 - Missing — no evidence, a complete lack of program and/or facility
NA - Not Applicable — not applicable to existing situation

Strengths, weaknesses, and immediate and long-range plans for improvement may be stated in the summary section at the end of the rating forms. This section will be particularly useful in effective program planning.

I. ADMINISTRATION OF THE MEDIA PROGRAM

AN EFFECTIVE MEDIA PROGRAM REQUIRES THE INVOLVEMENT, COMMITMENT, AND COOPERATION OF ADMINISTRATORS, TEACHERS, AND MEDIA STAFF.

Criteria:

	Available Check One			Utilization Check One				
	Yes	No	NA	1	2	3	4	5
1. The school's instructional team, composed of the principal, faculty, and media staff, jointly develop a unified media program.								
2. The media program is designed to meet the needs of individual students and teachers.								

		✕				

3. The school adminstration uses current state media guidelines in evaluating the media program, and providing personnel, facilities, budget, and equipment.

4. A system-level policy for the selection and acquisition of materials and equipment has been adopted by the local Board of Education.

5. The system-level selection policy has been filed with the Division of Educational Media, State Department of Public Instruction.

6. The system-level selection policy has been adapted to meet the needs of the school's instructional program.

7. The principal appoints a media advisory committee, chaired by the media coordinator, which reflects all academic insterests of the school.

8. The principal is responsible for the administration of the school media budget but plans the budget with the media advisory committee and authorizes the expenditure of funds.

9. Priorities for the allocation of media funds are based on both immediate needs and long-range goals of the school.

II. ACTIVITIES AND SERVICES

THE MEDIA PROGRAM ENCOMPASSES ALL SERVICES FOR PRINT, AUDIOVISUAL, AND TELEVISED MEDIA.

Criteria:

	Available Check One			Utilization Check One				
	Yes	No	NA	1	2	3	4	5
1. The media center strives to render services compatible with the stated philosophy and objectives of the school.								
2. The location and interior arrangement of the media center provide easy access to its services for all instructional areas.								
3. The media center has an "open door" policy and is available for individual student use before and after the regular school day.								
4. Flexible scheduling allows maximum use of all types of media simultaneously by individual students, small groups, and entire classes.								
5. Circulation policies make both materials and equipment readily available for a. individuals and classes b. materials for home use c. equipment for home use								

6. A sequential introduction to media skills (including use of all types of materials and equipment) has been developed jointly by teachers and the media coordinator.							
7. Media skills are taught jointly by the teacher and media coordinator.							
8. Large group instruction is reinforced with individualized instruction, projects and related activities.							
9. Instruction in media skills is a sequential process and is promoted to meet individual and/or grade-level needs.							
10. Students are encouraged to use the media production facilities and all types of media production equipment.							
11. The media staff secures materials for professional staff and students from the system-level center as well as from other sources.							

III. PERSONNEL

QUALIFIED PERSONNEL ARE ESSENTIAL TO AN EFFECTIVE MEDIA PROGRAM. THE MEDIA STAFF SHOULD BE COMPETENT IN THE USE OF PRINT, AUDIOVISUAL, AND TELEVISED MEDIA AND BE COGNIZANT OF LEARNING THEORY AND CURRICULUM DEVELOPMENT.

PERSONNEL NEEDS VARY ACCORDING TO STUDENT ENROLLMENT, PHYSICAL FACILITIES, AND THE SCOPE OF MEDIA SERVICES. EACH MEDIA CENTER SHOULD HAVE AT *LEAST ONE FULL-TIME*, CERTIFIED MEDIA PROFESSIONAL WITH A SUPPORT STAFF SUFFICIENT FOR THE CLERICAL AND TECHNICAL FUNCTIONS OF THE CENTER.

Criteria:

A. The Professional staff

1. A minimum of one media professional should be provided for an enrollment up to 999, two for an enrollment of 1000-1999, and three for 2000 to 2499. Rank your school:

   a. 1-499
   b. 500-999
   c. 1000-1999
   d. 2000-2499

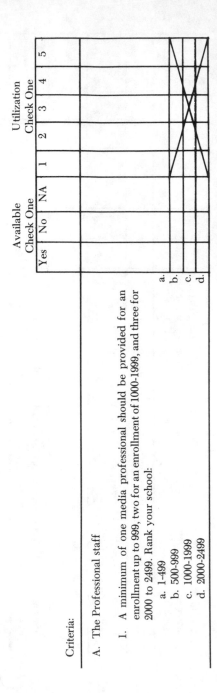

| | Available Check One | | Utilization Check One | | | | |
	Yes	No	NA	1	2	3	4	5
a.								
b.								
c.								
d.								

2. The media coordinator (chief professional):

   a. works enthusiastically and cooperatively with the professional staff and students keeping them fully informed about the media program;

   b. serves on curriculum development, textbook and other professional committees;

   c. is available for departmental and committee meetings on the nature and use of materials;

   d. chairs the media advisory committee;

   e. plans with the instructional team an integrated media program for all students;

   f. supervises the review, evaluation, selection, acquisition, and use of media in the school;

   g. communicates to superiors the quantitative and qualitative needs of the media program;

   h. selects and supervises student volunteers;

   i. selects and directs adult volunteers.

3. The professional staff:

   a. assists teachers in integrating media into instructional planning;

   b. maintains an active interest in the continuing developments of all aspects of educational media;

   c. is active in professional organizations;

   d. provides opportunities for inservice activities;

   e. assists the professional staff in the production of teacher-made materials;

   f. assists students in the production and utilization of media;

   g. publicizes the media collections and services in a variety of ways;

   h. locates available school television programs that relate to the curriculum and informs faculty;

   i. provides guidance in the making of video tape recordings of broadcast programs for later instructional use.

171

B. The Supporting Staff

1. A minimum of one paraprofessional is provided for an enrollment up to 499, two for an enrollment of 500-1499, and three for 1500 or more. Rank your school:
   - a. 1-499
   - b. 500-1499
   - c. 1500 or more

2. The supporting staff:
   - a. provides effective organization of materials and equipment for ease of use;
   - b. assists teachers in planning, designing, and producing materials to meet learning objectives when needed materials are not commercially available;
   - c. performs a variety of clerical and technical tasks to meet the interests and needs of individual students under the supervision of the media coordinator and/or classroom teacher.

	Available Check One			Utilization Check One				
	Yes	No	NA	1	2	3	4	5
a.								
b.								
c.								
a.								
b.								
c.								

IV. PHYSICAL FACILITIES

A. THE MEDIA CENTER

THE SCHOOL'S MEDIA FACILITIES SHOULD ENABLE MAXIMUM USE OF A FULL RANGE OF MATERIALS AND EQUIPMENT. THE MEDIA CENTER SHOULD BE CONVENIENT TO ALL CLASSROOMS. THE CENTER'S SIZE AND SPACE MUST ACCOMMODATE THE MEDIA PROGRAM'S RESOURCES, SERVICES, AND ACTIVITIES. SPACE FOR A MINIMUM OF 45 STUDENTS, OR 15% OF THE TOTAL ENROLLMENT (WHICHEVER IS LARGER), WITH 40 SQUARE FEET PER STUDENT TO READ, BROWSE, VIEW, AND LISTEN IS DESIRABLE.

ROOM FOR STORYTELLING IN ELEMENTARY SCHOOLS, FOR CONFERENCES, PROFESSIONAL MATERIALS, STORAGE, PRODUCTION, WORKROOM, AND OFFICES IS ADVISABLE. THE CENTER SHOULD HAVE AN INVITING ATMOSPHERE, ACOUSTICALLY TREATED WALLS AND FLOORS, GOOD LIGHTING, AND PROPER HEATING AND VENTILATION.

1. The media center is convenient to classrooms.								
2. The media center has easy access to the loading and delivery area.								
3. The media center has an inviting atmosphere which is conducive to learning.								
4. Arrangement of furniture promotes the effective use of the media center.								
5. The media center includes the following areas: . . . reading, browsing, circulation, and reference area accommodating a minimum of 45 students or 15% of total enrollment, whichever is larger; . . media multi-purpose room; . . listening and viewing areas; . . study carrel area; . . easily supervised conference areas; . . enclosed office; . . work area adjacent to office;								

173

Criteria: (continued)	Available Check One			Utilization Check One				
	Yes	No	NA	1	2	3	4	5
. . . storage facilities for equipment, supplies, and materials not immediately needed;								
. . . area for display and use of professional materials;								
. . . production facilities for producing audio and visual presentations;								
. . . facilities for video reception and recording;								
. . . storytelling area (elementary school only);								
. . . bulletin boards and display areas;								
. . . restroom facilities, nearby.								
6. The media center has sufficient								
a. light								
b. heat								
c. ventiliation.								
7. Walls are acoustically treated.								
8. Floor covering is sound absorbent.								
9. Storage facilities meet temperature and humidity requirements for certain audiovisual materials, equipment, and supplies.								

10. The media center provides the following:

... standard size, adjustable shelving;

... picture book dividers (elementary school only);

... periodical shelving;

... newspaper shelving;

... comfortable, casual furniture;

... tables and chairs of suitable size and height;

... dictionary stand;

... atlas stand;

... card catalog and shelf list cabinets;

... proper storage facilities for each type of nonprint material;

... book trucks;

Criteria: (continued)	Available Check One			Utilization Check One				
	Yes	No	NA	1	2	3	4	5
. . . audiovisual equipment carts;								
. . . sink with running water;								
. . . electrically-wired study carrels (wet);								
. . . unwired study carrels (dry);								
. . . circulation desk;								
. . . typewriter.								
11. The media center has adequate electric power and outlets to accommodate all media activites.								

B. TEACHING/LEARNING AREAS

ALTHOUGH THE MEDIA CENTER IS THE NUCLEUS OF THE MEDIA FACILITIES, ALL TEACHING/LEARNING AREAS SHOULD ACCOMMODATE THE FULL USE OF ALL MEDIA. FURNISHINGS SHOULD ENCOURAGE FLEXIBLE ARRANGEMENT AND USE.

Criteria:

	Available Check One			Utilization Check One				
	Yes	No	NA	1	2	3	4	5
1. Each learning area has:								
a. sufficient artificial and natural light control,								
b. acoustically treated floors and walls,								
c. properly spaced electrical outlets.								
2. Each learning area contains adequate storage facilities for equipment and materials.								
3. Projection screens are available for every learning area.								
4. Building design permits easy transportation of audiovisual equipment and materials.								
5. Building design permits use of television from master antenna system.								

V. LEARNING RESOURCES

THE MEDIA COLLECTION IS ONE ESSENTIAL COMPONENT OF THE MEDIA PROGRAM *BUT DOES NOT CONSTITUTE A PROGRAM.* THE COLLECTION SHOULD INCLUDE A VARIETY OF CAREFULLY SELECTED MATERIALS AND EQUIPMENT IN VARIOUS FORMATS SUFFICIENT IN DEPTH AND SCOPE TO MEET INSTRUCTIONAL NEEDS AS WELL AS INTERESTS, AND ABILITY LEVELS OF STUDENTS.

A. THE COLLECTION

Criteria:

	Available Check One			Utilization Check One				
	Yes	No	NA	1	2	3	4	5
1. A comprehensive collection includes:								
. . . (a) newspapers (national, state, local)	a.							
. . . (b) periodicals representing different editorial viewpoints and providing wide coverage;	b.							
. . . back issues (at least 3 years back) of periodicals indexed in the ABRIDGED READER'S GUIDE:								
. . . books: levels I=12 books per student Level II=14 books per student Level III=18 and up per student;								

							Item
							. . . reference collection;
							. . . a wide range of audio, visual, and other non-print media.
							2. An organized, updated, and accessible information file is available.
							3. A relevant print and non-print professional collection serves staff development needs.
							4. An adequate and appropriate balance of materials and equipment is evident.
							5. A variety of materials, equipment, and supplies enables the production of educational media unavailable from commercial sources.
							6. Sufficient audiovisual equipment is available to avoid inconvenience and delay.
							7. An adequate number of television receivers, providing good reception, is available.
							8. A file of teachers guides and schedules to series offered through School Television is available.
							9. A file of community resources (persons, places, and things) is available.

B. SELECTION, ORGANIZATION AND MANAGEMENT OF THE COLLECTION

	Available Check One			Utilization Check One				
Criteria:	Yes	No	NA	1	2	3	4	5
1. All educational media of permanent value regardless of where they are housed and how acquired are inventoried, classified, and cataloged centrally.								
2. Inventory procedures and records of the media collection serve the Media Advisory Committee as an excellent guide in setting priorities for the selection and acquisition of media.								
3. The instructional staff assists the media coordinator in selecting new materials and in weeding existing collections.								
4. Recommened selection tools, including advisory lists are used in the selection of media.								
5. Media orders for replacements, subscriptions, and requested materials are placed in the spring for early delivery, with remaining purchases made throughout the year as needs dictate.								
6. Systematic ordering procedures are used.								

180

7. A card catalog of all educational media provides accessibility to the media whether commercially acquired or locally produced.						
8. The shelf list includes information about the acquisition of all materials.						
9. All media are subject to occasional inspection and to systematic weeding.						
10. The media budget provides for the acquisition of sufficient materials and equipment to meet instructional needs.						
11. The media advisory committee is periodically informed of the media budget balance(s) by the administration.						
12. Consideration is given to the budgeting of funds for the maintenance of media such as the rebinding of books and the repairing of equipment.						
13. Priorities are set by the media advisory committee for the expenditure of federal, state and local funds for the acquisition of material and equipment.						

VI. SUMMARY
A. Areas of Strength:

B. Areas of Weakness:

C. Immediate Plans of Improvement:

D. Long-range Plans for Improvement:

E

AN INSTRUMENT FOR THE SELF-EVALUATION OF TEACHERS AND MEDIA SPECIALISTS

FEATURES CHARACTERIZING THE MEDIA CENTER AND CORRESPONDING BEHAVIORS OF TEACHERS AND MEDIA SPECIALISTS

I. *THE ATMOSPHERE OF THE MEDIA CENTER IS COMPOUNDED OF: EASY ACCESSIBILITY, FLEXIBLE ADMINISTRATION, PHYSICAL ATTRACTIVENESS, EMOTIONAL WARMTH.*

TEACHER BEHAVIORS:

_____The teacher enjoys approaching the librarian at any time for help with materials, with unit planning, or with student problems.

_____The teacher feels free to send individuals and groups to the library from his classroom.

_____The teacher brings his class to the library as needed rather than on a rigid schedule.

_____The teacher is able to borrow any materials for use in his classroom.

_____The teacher feels free to plan many innovations in the use of materials.

_____The teacher has the opportunity of bringing his class often for activities which he has planned with the librarian.

_____The teacher visits the library before and after school or during the day to plan with the librarian and to gather or review materials.

_____The teacher finds that he has a voice in changing library regulations which he finds limit the use of the library.

MEDIA SPECIALIST OR LIBRARIAN BEHAVIORS:

_____The librarian makes every effort to meet teacher and student needs at all times.

_____The librarian exhibits a pleasant, friendly, accepting attitude toward teachers and students.

_____The librarian demonstrates much enthusiasm in his work.

_____The librarian adopts an "open" policy in the administration of the library so that students are not kept out by rigid rules and regulations.

_____The librarian adds many decorative touches to make the library an inviting place.

_____The librarian keeps the library open before and after school as well as during the school day. The library may also be kept open at night or on weekends.

_____The librarian promotes an informal atmosphere in the library.

_____The librarian is glad to change any regulation which is found to be against the best interests of teachers or students.

_____The librarian is receptive to innovative teaching methods which involve changes in the way the library is used.

_____The librarian encourages the circulation of all library materials to classrooms and homes.

_____The librarian is quick to add to the library collection any new media.

_____The librarian cooperates with changing utilization of staff and offers to serve as a member of teaching teams.

_____The librarian encourages the use of the library by individuals and small groups coming from study halls and/or classrooms.

_____The librarian works with teachers and principals to develop a flexible scheduling of classes to the library.

II. THE MEDIA CENTER SERVES AS A CENTRALIZED MULTI-MEDIA RESOURCE.

TEACHER BEHAVIORS:

_____The teacher knows the contributions which all types of media can make to his teaching, and makes effective use of the media most appropriate for a specific purpose.

_____The teacher takes steps to remedy any "blind spots" in his understanding of how to use new equipment and media.

_____The teacher varies his teaching methods to take advantage of new teaching tools.

_____The teacher often consults the librarian in his capacity of media specialist.

_____The teacher becomes familiar with the library materials in his respective field.

_____The teacher works with the librarian to improve and increase the collection of materials he uses.

184

MEDIA SPECIALIST OR LIBRARIAN BEHAVIORS:

_____The librarian is thoroughly familiar with the school curriculum, with teaching methods and with student, faculty, and community interests so that he can develop an excellent functional collection of materials.

_____The librarian organizes all materials for quick and easy access. He catalogs and inventories materials which are on permanent loan to departments and classrooms.

_____The librarian serves as a media specialist and spends much time becoming familiar with the content of all media in the library.

_____The librarian provides materials for the atypical student, the slow learning, the gifted, the non-verbal, culturally disadvantaged, etc.

_____The librarian knows and keeps on hand the approved selection aids for all media and orders new materials only after consulting these lists and/or after personal examination.

_____The librarian with the teacher's help weeds the collection frequently to discard out-of-date and out-worn materials.

_____The librarian urges that all supplementary instructional materials be selected, ordered, and inventoried through the library.

III. THE MEDIA CENTER SERVES AS A LEARNING LABORATORY WHICH IMPLEMENTS THE GOALS OF THE TOTAL SCHOOL PROGRAM.

TEACHER BEHAVIORS:

_____The teacher regards the library as part of his classroom.

_____The teacher uses the librarian's services and the library equipment in the construction of teaching materials.

_____The teacher plans library activities which are an outgrowth of his instructional program.

_____The teachers plans with the librarian activities to promote critical thinking and reading.

_____The teacher implements an easy two-way flow of materials and services between library and classroom.

_____The teacher makes use of materials and librarian services for exceptional students, the slow learners, the gifted, and other atypical students.

_____The teacher plans with the librarian on a continuous basis.

_____The teacher in cooperation with the librarian teaches library skills and provides many opportunities for their use.

_____The teacher sends to the librarian for instruction those individuals or small groups needing special help with some skill.

_____The teacher often works in the library with her class.

_____The teacher requests the services of the librarian in the classroom.

_____The teacher plans with the librarian ways to help students grow in their knowledge of great literature.

_____The teacher plans library activities to promote independent student work-habits and learning.

MEDIA SPECIALIST OR LIBRARIAN BEHAVIORS:

_____The librarian maintains good working relations with all staff members.

_____The librarian considers technical and routine duties subordinate to working with teachers and students.

_____The librarian serves on curriculum committees.

_____The librarian assists teachers and students in the contruction of teaching materials.

_____The librarian keeps informed concerning classroom activities.

_____The librarian, individually and in departmental meetings, plans with teachers.

_____The librarian encourages students to become independent in their use of the library materials and teaches library skills cooperatively with teachers as the need arises for their use.

_____The librarian extends her services into the classroom teaching library skills, giving book talks, and finding ways to intergrate the use of print and non-print materials.

_____The librarian requests the facilities for independent use of the library and for expanded services.

_____The librarian keeps students and teachers informed of new materials received and innovations in library services and educational practices.

_____The librarian provides materials and helps plan programs to promote the professional growth of the school staff.

_____The librarian works individually with students helping them define a field of inquiry, locate information, and evaluate data which is pertinent.

IV. *THE MEDIA CENTER SERVES AN AN AGENCY TO PROMOTE THE STUDENT'S PERSONAL DEVELOPMENT.*

TEACHER BEHAVIORS:

_____The teacher in her guidance role consults with the librarian in the development of desirable student habits and attitudes.

_____The teacher plans with the librarian many creative activities to establish permanent reading habits, and to raise tastes in the areas of listening, viewing, and reading.

_____The teacher plans with the librarian ways to broaden student interests and to enrich their experiential background.

_____The teacher uses a policy of encouragement and stimulation to help students discover the joys of reading.

_____The teacher consults the librarian often for advice on the most appropriate books for certain students.

_____The teacher always seeks to relate the use of books and other media to the concerns and problems of youth to foster a life-long interest in learning.

_____The teacher directs students to the library's collection of vocational and guidance materials.

_____The teachers asks the librarian to assist in evaluating the student's library work-habits.

_____The teacher plans activities to develop good listening and viewing skills.

_____The teacher uses library resources to guide students in the appreciation of great art and music.

_____The teacher infects her class with her enthusiasm about reading.

_____The teacher becomes informed about the books being written for young people today which reflect their interests and problems.

MEDIA SPECIALIST OR LIBRARIAN BEHAVIORS:

_____The librarian publicizes library services and materials in many inventive attractive ways which are related to student interests and mores.

_____The librarian has a part in the guidance program, consulting with counselors and teachers, advising students, and making up-to-date vocational and guidance materials available.

_____The librarian works with teachers to help students form good listening and viewing habits and to develop criteria for the evaluation of mass media.

_____The librarian suggests to teachers a variety of ways for students to share their reading.

_____The librarian introduces students individually and in groups progressively to a higher quality of reading.

_____The librarian works with teachers to develop lists of books to serve as suggestions for students selections.

_____The librarian helps students through their use of the library, a communal facility, to develop an understanding of the duties, rights, and privileges of a citizen.

_____The librarian values the worth of each student and helps him develop a strong self-concept.

_____The librarian gives students the opportunity to serve as library assistants.

_____The librarian provides materials and develops activities to raise tastes in the areas of art and music.

In the space before each statement, place a number rating yourself on the following scale:

1-Poor
2-Fair
3-Good
4-Excellent

Total your scores.

TEACHERS

120-156 - You're making excellent use of the media center.

80-119 - Your're making good use of the media center but are missing some services.

45-79 - The media center could contribute twice as much to your instructional program.

1-44 - The media center is having practically no impact on your instructional program.

LIBRARIANS

135-172 - An excellent program has been developed.

90-134 - The program is good but other services could be developed.

45-89 - The range of services could be doubled.

1-44 - The program is just beginning to be developed.

F

School District
of Greenville County
Division of Library Service
Secondary School Libraries
Annual Report 1971-1972

This evaluation is based on the objectives chosen by the Program Committee of the Secondary School Librarians' Group for the school year 1971-1972. The objectives are as follows:

Librarians will become informed concerning new programs in the district and new educational trends in general.

New materials and services will be added to libraries for the culturally different students.

The librarian will consider each child worthy of respect and entitled to individualized service.

Check activities you engaged in this year which helped you to become informed about new programs in the district and new educational trends in general.

( ) Workshops
( ) Visits to other schools
( ) College courses
( ) Reading
( ) Programs of county and state organizations
( ) Experiments with new programs
( ) Other

Check materials and services which have been added or significantly increased for the culturally different students. Also check the appropriate columns to show how much use was made of these materials.

ESTIMATE OF USE

	Excellent	Good	Fair	Poor

Materials added:

( ) Filmstrips
( ) Sound filmstrips (coordinated record and filmstrip)
( ) Paperback books
( ) Recordings
( ) Magazines
( ) Games
( ) Consummable materials for creative acitivites ("U" film transparency pens & colored acetate, etc., blank cassettes, crayons, paint, etc.)
( ) Black studies materials
( ) Corrective reading materials
( ) Enrichment printed materials for students reading below grade level
( ) Other_____

Services Added:

( ) Working individually with students
( ) Planning with teachers for special learning activities
( ) Special filmstrip activities for groups or individuals
( ) Providing opportunities for students to play educational games and work puzzles
( ) Encouraging creative activities with all media
( ) Developing displays on Black leaders and history
( ) Reading guidance
( ) Providing for the use of specialized reading materials
( ) Working on paperback books with groups
( ) Other_____

To aid in future evaluation of progress in teacher-librarian planning, give the number of teachers with whom you held regular planning sessions at least once a month this school year_____

191

The Annual Report Committee felt that the best way to determine whether students are treated as individuals and with respect is to ask the students themselves. Therefore, we have compiled the following questionnaire to be distributed by teachers to three students in each English class. Select the first, twelfth, and last student on the class roll. Duplicate the attached questionnaire for your English teachers, distribute and collect them. Compile the answers below.

SUMMARY OF RESPONSES TO STUDENT QUESTIONNAIRE: (Hold for Annual Report)

Total number of responses _____

1. How often do you go to the library?
   Several times a week _____ Once a week _____ Twice a month _____
   Once a month _____ Less than once a month _____

2. Do you look at filmstrips in the library?
   Often _____ Occasionally _____ Never _____

3. Do you listen to records or cassettes in the library?
   Often _____ Occasionally _____ Never _____

4. Do you use the card catalog?
   Often _____ Occasionally _____ Never _____

5. Do you use the Reader's Guide?
   Often _____ Occasionally _____ Never _____

6. Do the librarians and assistants give you the assistance you need to find books and materials?
   Often _____ Occasionally _____ Never _____

192

7. Are you able to find the materials you need?
   Yes_____ Sometimes_____ No_____

8. Do you enjoy going to the library? Yes_____ Sometimes_____ No_____

9. Do you go to the library when you need to from classrooms?
   Yes_____ No_____

10. Why do you usually go to the library?
    Recreational reading_____ Reference work_____ Checking out books_____
    Viewing and listening activities_____ Other_____

11. The library is too quiet_____ too noisy_____ all right_____

12. List any additional materials or activities you would like in the library.

    _____

    _____

13. List any suggestions you have for improving student use of the library.

    _____

    _____

G

LIBRARY SERVICES SURVEY CHECKLIST

SCHOOL———————————

HOW DO YOU RATE YOUR LIBRARY SERVICES
IN COMPARISON WITH NATIONAL STANDARDS?

Evaluate according to the categories listed below:

Reading, Listening, and Viewing Guidance

	POOR	FAIR	GOOD	EXCELLENT
Cooperative planning and work with teachers				
Meeting individual needs and interests of pupils				
Meeting class needs				
Cooperative work with special teachers				
Providing materials for special readers (Gifted or deprived)				
Guidance by book displays, book talks, story telling, reading aloud, etc.				
Instruction in listening and viewing				

	POOR	FAIR	GOOD	EXCELLENT
Meeting audio-visual material needs of classes				
Meeting audio-visual material needs of special pupils (gifted or deprived)				
Guidance in the selection and use of films, filmstrips, recordings, television programs				
Guidance in the selection and use of reference materials				

Reference Services

	POOR	FAIR	GOOD	EXCELLENT
Visits to the library by teachers with their classes:				
Frequency				
Effectiveness				
Visits to the Library by individuals:				
Frequency				
Effectiveness				
Visits to the library by small groups from classrooms				
Frequency				
Effectiveness				

Use of Variety of Materials

	POOR	FAIR	GOOD	EXCELLENT
Films				
Filmstrips				
Loops				
Transparencies				
Tapes				
Records				
Mounted Pictures				
Printed materials				

Instruction in The Use of The Library

	POOR	FAIR	GOOD	EXCELLENT
Use of new techniques and media (Transparencies, films, tapes, etc)				
Teacher-Librarian Planning				
Instruction by teachers				

	POOR	FAIR	GOOD	EXCELLENT
Appropiate materials and correlation with instructional program				
Individualized instruction by librarian				
Small group instruction by librarian				
Effectiveness of orientation lessons				

Student Assistants

	POOR	FAIR	GOOD	EXCELLENT
Selection procedures				
Contribution to Library Program				
Dependability				
Degree of Personal Development Fostered				
Amount of Recognition for Services				

Personal and Social Guidance

	POOR	FAIR	GOOD	EXCELLENT
Adequacy of Materials for Guidance				
Development of Student Responsibility				
Development of Student Respect for Rights of Others				
Frequency of Conferences with Individuals				
Promotion of Vocational Guidance Materials				
Development of Student Ability to Work Independently				
Development of Student Ability to Work Well With Others				

Assistance to Teachers and Students in The Construction of Teaching Materials

	POOR	FAIR	GOOD	EXCELLENT
Equipment available				
Working space available				
Staff available				
Degree of assistance				

H

Library Evaluation
by Principals

Objective: *Each child develops the knowledge that the library has an important place in his life.*

1. The library should have a warm and inviting atmosphere. How would you rate the atmosphere of your library?
   Poor_____ Fair_____ Good_____ Excellent_____
2. How would you rate the librarian-pupil relationships?
   Poor_____ Fair_____ Good_____ Excellent_____
3. Is the library easily accessible before, during and after school?
   Never_____ Sometimes_____ Often_____ Very Often_____
4. Estimate how often children voluntarily pursue their personal interests in the library.
   Never_____ Sometimes_____ Often_____ Very Often_____

Objective: *Teachers and librarians work together to help each child select books on their reading levels and interests.*

1. Do teachers and librarians work together in the library to help children select books?
   Never_____ Seldom_____ Often_____ Always_____
2. Do teachers keep librarians informed of childrens' reading levels?
   Never_____ Seldom_____ Often_____ Always_____

197

3. How would you evaluate the extent to which teachers and librarians know children and their interests?
Poor_____ Fair_____ good_____ Excellent_____
4. How would you evaluate the extent to which the librarian knows the book collection?
Poor_____ Fair_____ Good_____ Excellent_____

OBJECTIVE: *The librarian interprets to teachers the ways in which the library can promote and enrich each student's learning.*

1. Does the librarian inform teachers of new materials as they are acquired?
Never_____ Seldom_____ Often_____ Always_____
2. Does the librarian meet with the faculty in curriculum planning or other meetings?
Never_____ Seldom_____ Often_____ Always_____
3. Do the teachers plan *continuously* with the librarian for effective use of materials?
Never_____ Seldom_____ Often_____ Always_____
4. Do teachers keep librarians informed concerning units of study and class needs?
Never_____ Seldom_____ Often_____ Always_____

OBJECTIVE: *Facilities are provided in the library for individualized and small group use of non-book material.*

1. Are children taught to use all types of A-V equipment?
Not at all_____ Sometimes_____ Often_____
Very Often_____
2. Are teachers encouraging independent use of A-V resources by individual or small groups?
Not at all_____ Sometimes_____ Often_____
Very Often_____
3. How would you rate the space and equipment which has been provided in the library for using A-V materials?
Poor_____ Fair_____ Good_____ Excellent_____

I

STUDENT EVALUATION OF LIBRARY MEDIA CENTER

Check approximately how many hours you came to the library last month:*

	No. Times Checked		No. Times Checked
0	_____	10 - 14	_____
1 - 4	_____	15 - 20	_____
5 - 9	_____	over 20	_____

If you did not come to the library as much as you wanted to, state the reason:

_____

_____

_____

_____

_____

How many times last month did you use the library to find information on subjects?

	No. Times Checked		No. Times Checked
0 - 0	_____	10 - 14	_____
1 - 4	_____	15 - 20	_____
5 - 9	_____		

*Each librarian in thirty-four schools compiled the answers on the questionnaires.

How many times last month did you use the library for reading for pleasure?

	No. Times Checked		No. Times Checked
0	_____	10 - 14	_____
1 - 4	_____	15 - 20	_____
5 - 9	_____		

How many times did you need assistance in locating information in the library:

	No. times Checked		No. Times Checked
0	_____	10 - 14	_____
1 - 4	_____	15 - 20	_____

How many times did you need assistance in locating information in the library:

(Cont.)

	No. Times Checked
5 - 9	_____

Approximately how many books, not required for classwork, have you read in the past month?

	No. Times Checked		No. Times Checked
0	_____	10 - 14	_____
1 - 4	_____	15 - 20	_____
5 - 9	_____		

How many times did you think you needed further instruction in how to use the library?

	No. Times Checked		No. Times Checked
Not at all	_____	Very Often	_____
Sometimes	_____	All the time	_____
Frequently	_____		

How often does the librarian help you?

	No. Times Checked		No. Times Checked
Not at all	_____	Very often	_____
Sometimes	_____	All the time	_____
Frequently	_____		

Do you find enough of the following materials available?

	No. Times Checked YES	No. Times Checked NO
Filmstrips	_____	_____
Recordings	_____	_____
Mounted Pictures	_____	_____
Pamphlets	_____	_____
Periodicals	_____	_____

How do you rate te services of the student library assistants?

	No. Times Checked		No. Times Checked
Very Poor	_____	Good	_____
Poor	_____	Excellent	_____
Fair	_____		

Check the activities which helped you find the books you wanted to read:

	No. Times Checked
1. Book talks by librarian	_____
2. Book displays in library	_____
3. Recommendations by another student	_____
4. Notices in school paper	_____

5. Teacher suggestions (not required reading)   —————

6. Other (Specify)   —————

List on suggestion as to how the library could serve you better:

_____

_____

_____

_____

_____

BIBLIOGRAPHY

1. ALFONSO, Robert J. Instructional Supervision; a Behavior System. Boston, Allyn and Bacon, Incorporated, 1975.
2. AMERICAN ASSOCIATION OF SCHOOL LIBRARIANS AND THE DEPARTMENT OF AUDIO-VISUAL INSTRUCTION OF THE NATIONAL EDUCATION ASSOCIATION. Standards for School Media Programs, Chicago, American Library Association, 1969.
3. AMERICAN ASSOCIATION OF SCHOOL LIBRARIANS. Standards for School Library Programs. Chicago, American Library Association, 1960.
4. BAKER, D. Phillip, School and Public Library Media Programs for Children and Young Adults. Syracuse, New York, Gaylord Professional Publications, 1977.
5. BOMAR, Cora Paul, M. Ann HEIDBREDER, and Carol A. NEMEYER. Guide to the Development of Educational Media Selection Centers. (ALA Studies in Librarianship, Number 4). Chicago, American Library Association, 1973.
6. BOWDEN, M. G. "The Principal and the School Librarian." *Wilson Library Bulletin,* 37:592, March, 1963.
7. DARLING, Richard L. Teams for Better Education; the Teacher and the Librarian. Champaign, Illinois, Garrard Publishing Company, nd.

8. DAVIES, Ruth Ann, The School Library, a Force for Educational Excellence. New York, R.R. Bowker Company, 1969.
9. DERTHICK, Lawrence G. "You and the Administrator." *Library Journal*, 87:4234, November 15, 1962.
10. DOLL, Ronald C. Curriculum Improvement: Decision Making in Process. Boston, Allyn and Bacon, Inc., 1970.
11. ELSEROAD, Homer O. "The Superintendent's Key Role in Improving School Libraries." *School Principals Bulletin*, 50:1-5, January, 1966.
12. ERICKSON, Carlton W.H. Administering Instructional Media Programs. New York, The MacMillan Company, 1968.
13. FINCH, Mildred E. "Improving Working Relationships: The Media Specialist and the School Administrator." Southeastern Librarian, 21:222-25, Winter, 1971.
14. FITE, A.E. "Librarians and Administrators: Working Toward a Common Goal." *Hoosier School Librarian*, 15:15-18, December, 1975.
15. GAVER, Mary Virginia. Services of Secondary School Media Centers; Evaluation and Development. Chicago, American Library Association, 1971.
16. GILLESPIE, John and Diane L. SPIRT. Creating a School Media Program. New York, R.R. Bowker Company, 1973.
17. GLASSER, Joyce Fern. The Elementary School Learning Center for Independent Study. West Nyack, New York. Parker Publishing Company, 1971.
18. GOODLAD, John I. Principals Are the Key to Change. Education Digest, 42:32-5, November, 1976.
19. HUGE, J. "Principal as a Staff Development Leader." *Educational* Leadership, 34:384-6, February, 1977.
20. KEARNEY, J. "Principal: Teacher of Teachers." *National Association of Secondary School Principals Bulletin*, 61:1-6, February, 1977.
21. KESTRA, G. "We Did It 'My Way' - Right or Wrong." *Illinois Librarian*, 58:565-7, September, 1976.
22. KIRST, Michael W. Politics of Education at the Local, State and Federal Levels. Berkley, California, McCutchan Publishing Company, 1970.

23. LIESENER, James W. A Systematic Process For Planning Media Programs. Chicago, American Library Association, 1976.
24. LOERTSCHER David V. and Janet G. STROUD. Purdue Self-Evaluation Instrument for School Media Centers. West Lafayette, Indiana, Purdue Research Foundation, 1976.
25. LICATA, Joseph W. "In the School's Social System is the Principal an Effective Change Agent?" *National Association of Secondary School Principals Bulletin,* 59:91-4, December, 1975.
26. LOGSDON, James V. and V.M. KERENSKY. "The Principal's Responsibilities in Community Education." *National Association of Secondary School* Principals Bulletin, 59:1-4, November, 1975.
27. Media Programs, District and School. Prepared by the American Association of School Libraries, American Library Association and Association for Educational Communications and Technology. Chicago, American Library Association and Washington, Association for Educational Communications and Technology, 1975.
28. McGINNISS, Dorothy. "Administrator and Librarian Work Together." *Wisconsin Library Bulletin,* 42:211, July, 1966.
29. Nebraska Guide for Establishing, Developing, Evaluating School Media Programs. Carson City, Nebraska State Department of Education, 1975.
30. McNEIL, John D. Curriculum; a Comprehensive Introduction. Boston, Little, Brown and Company, 1977.
31. Policies and Procedures for Selection of Instructional Materials. Chicago, American Association of School Librarians, 1970.
32. PROSTANO, Emanuel T. and Joyce S. PROSTANO. The School Library Media Center. Littleton, Colorado, Librarian Unlimited, Incorporated, 1971.
33. ROGUS, J. and T. MATEZYNSKI. "Principal - Central Office Communication." *National Association of Secondary School Principals Bulletin,* 61:37-43, January, 1977.

34. Rossoff, Martin. The School Library and Educational Change. Littleton, Colorado, Libraries Unlimited, Inc., 1971.

35. Rowell, J.A. New Standards and the Administrator. New York, Bowker Annual of Library and Book Trade Information, 1970.

36. Saunders, Helen E. The Modern School Library. Metuchen, New Jersey, Scarecrow Press, 1968.

37. Schwilch, Gene L. "The Library Needs the Principal." *National Association of Secondary School Principals Bulletin*, 50:6-9, January, 1966.

38. Southern States Work Conference Committee. Achieving Quality in School Library Service. Tallahassee, Florida State Department of Education, nd.

39. Stoops, Emery, Max Rafferty and Russell E. Johnson. Handbook of Educational Administration; A Guide for the Practitioner. Boston, Allyn and Bacon, 1975.

40. Swarthout, Charlene R. "The School Library as Part of the Instructional System. Metuchen, New Jersey, The Scarecrow Press, 1967.

41. Walraven, Margaret Kessler and Arthur Hallguest. Teaching Through the Elementary School Library. New York, H.W. Wilson Company, 1948.

42. Ward, Pearl L. and Robert Bacon, comp. The School Media Center; a Book of Readings. Metuchen, New Jersey, Scarecrow Press, 1973.

Index